Physical Cha...
Curly-Co...

(from the American Kennel Club breed standard)

Body: Chest is decidedly deep and not too wide, oval in cross-section, with brisket reaching elbow. The ribs are well-sprung, neither barrel-shaped nor slab-sided, and extend well back into a deep, powerful loin with a moderate tuck-up of flank.

Hindquarters: Strong and in balance with front angulation. Thighs are powerful with muscling carrying well down into the second thigh. Stifle is of moderate bend. The hocks are strong and true.

Tail: Carried straight or fairly straight, never docked and reaching approximately to the hock.

Coat: The body coat is a thick mass of small, tight, crisp curls, lying close to the skin, resilient, water resistant and of sufficient density to provide protection against weather, water and punishing cover. Curls also extend up the entire neck to the occiput, down the thigh and back leg to at least the hock and over the entire tail. Elsewhere, the coat is short, smooth and straight, including on the forehead, face, front of forelegs and feet.

Size: Dogs, 25 to 27 inches; bitches, 23 to 25 inches.

Color: Black or liver. Either color is correct.

Curly-Coated Retriever

By Nona Kilgore Bauer

Contents

9   **History of the** Curly-Coated Retriever

Discover the origins of this most ancient of retriever breeds, whose origins are submerged in 15th-century Britain. Trace the development of this unique water retriever with tremendous swimming and hunting power from Britain to Australia and New Zealand, where the breed has a significant following, to the US, where the breed is just beginning to establish a stronghold.

21 **Characteristics of the** Curly-Coated Retriever

Underneath the Curly's unique coat of crisp, tight curls is a dog equally unique—meet the independent and intelligent Curly-Coated Retriever. Find out about the breed's personality and trainability as well as its physical characteristics, including the possible hereditary conditions of which all owners should be aware.

33 **Breed Standard for the** Curly-Coated Retriever

Learn the requirements of a well-bred Curly-Coated Retriever by studying the description of the breed set forth in the American Kennel Club standard. Both show dogs and pets must possess key characteristics as outlined in the breed standard.

39   **Your Puppy** Curly-Coated Retriever

Find out about how to locate a well-bred Curly-Coated Retriever puppy. Discover which questions to ask the breeder and what to expect when visiting the litter. Prepare for your puppy-accessory shopping spree. Also discussed are home safety, the first trip to the vet, socialization and solving basic puppy problems.

67 **Proper Care of Your** Curly-Coated Retriever

Cover the specifics of taking care of your Curly-Coated Retriever every day: feeding for all life stages; grooming, including coat care, ears, eyes, nails and bathing; and exercise needs. Also discussed are dog ID and traveling safely with your dog.

Training Your Curly-Coated Retriever   85

Begin with the basics of training the puppy and adult dog. Learn the principles of house-training the Curly-Coated Retriever, including the use of crates and basic scent instincts. Get started by introducing the pup to his collar and leash and progress to the basic commands. Find out about obedience classes and other activities.

Healthcare of Your Curly-Coated Retriever   110

By Lowell Ackerman DVM, DACVD
Become your dog's healthcare advocate and a well-educated canine keeper. Select a skilled and able veterinarian. Discuss pet insurance, vaccinations and infectious diseases, the neuter/spay decision and a sensible, effective plan for parasite control, including fleas, ticks and worms.

Your Senior Curly-Coated Retriever   139

Know when to consider your Curly-Coated Retriever a senior and what special needs he will have. Learn to recognize the signs of aging in terms of physical and behavioral traits and what your vet can do to optimize your dog's golden years.

Showing Your Curly-Coated Retriever   146

Enter the world of showing pure-bred dogs. Acquaint yourself with the basics of AKC conformation showing, including how to get started, how shows are organized and how a dog becomes a champion. Take a leap into other competitive events suitable for the Curly: obedience and agility trials, tracking tests, field trials and hunting events.

Index 156

Photography by Carol Ann Johnson and Michael Trafford
with additional photographs by

John Ashbey, Peter Atkinson, Norvia Behling, Booth by Monica, Paulette Braun, Alan and Sandy Carey, Carolina Biological Supply, Susan Chow, Isabelle Français, Javan, Bill Jonas, Dr. Dennis Kunkel, Paul Lepiane, Gary & Mary Meek, Tam C. Nguyen, Phototake, Jean Claude Revy, Kitten Rodwell, Stewart Event Images, Tatham and Alice van Kempen.

Illustrations by Rénée Low and Patricia Peters.

The publisher wishes to thank all of the owners whose dogs are featured in this book, including Susan Chow, Conrad & Anne Clippert, Yvonne Cooper, Gary & Mary Meek, John Mello, Audrey Nicholls, Hayden & Gladys Phillips, Nicola Phillips-McFarlane and Sue Tokolics.

KENNEL CLUB BOOKS® CURLY-COATED RETRIEVER
ISBN: 1-59378-318-3

Copyright © 2006 • Kennel Club Books, LLC
308 Main Street, Allenhurst, NJ 07711 USA
Cover Design Patented: US 6,435,559 B2 • Printed in South Korea

10 9 8 7 6 5 4 3 2 1

The Curly-Coated Retriever possesses many unique features in both looks and personality that set him apart from the other retriever breeds.

HISTORY OF THE
CURLY-COATED RETRIEVER

The Curly-Coated Retriever is considered the most unique of all of the retriever breeds. With his sturdy legs and body covered in a mass of tight shiny curls, he appears more to be a cuddly teddy bear than a capable and courageous hunting dog. He is also the least recognized of the retrievers and is often mistaken for the Poodle or the Irish Water Spaniel, his distant relatives of centuries ago. Although the Curly is a most popular gundog in New Zealand and Australia, where he is prized for his strength, courage and tenacity, the breed is not very well known in the United States and many other parts of the world.

ORIGIN AND ESTABLISHMENT OF THE BREED IN ENGLAND

Unlike the histories of the other retriever breeds, few specifics are known about the history and development of the Curly in his native England. However, pre-1800 writings do offer valid evidence of the breed's existence centuries earlier; references dating back to the 15th century describe "sagacious" curly-coated spaniels and water dogs who possessed outstanding hunting and retrieving ability. Author Phillip Ashburton wrote about Curly-Coated Retrievers used for hunting around 1490 in Lincolnshire and Norfolk, the land of Robin Hood and his merry band. Centuries later, a reference in the *Sportsman's Cabinet* in 1803 suggested that the Curly is a descendant of the "Old Water Dog" with the following: "These dogs are exceedingly angular in appearance and most probably derived their origin from the Greenland dog blended with some particular race of their own. The hair of these dogs must be adhering to the body in natural elastic curls, not loose or long and shaggy."

Subsequent documentation from the mid-1800s offers several

The Curly-Coat is an able land and water retriever. Rebel, the only Best in Show Curly in the US also to have earned an AKC hunting title, beautifully embodies the breed's natural aptitude in the field.

A Curly-Coated Retriever from the early 1900s.

other accounts of the Curly's place in evolution as a gundog in England. Writer John Scott wrote in 1820 in the *Sportsman's Repository*, "The original Water Dog of the opposite continent, being long since adopted in this country and in some maritime districts, is still preserved in a state of purity, but the breed is more generally intermixed with the Water Spaniel and Newfoundland Dog."

Most breed historians assume that the St. John's Newfoundland, the Tweed Water Spaniel, the Irish Water Spaniel and the Poodle may have contributed to the development of the Curly-Coated Retriever in England. Because all of these breeds were evolving at about the same time, it is also possible that the reverse is true and the Curly is the dominant link behind the development of those other breeds.

Some authorities believe that the Curly-Coated Retriever was crossed with the original Poodle of Germany, with the goal of improving the coat and elegance of the Curly and the staying power and sagacity of the Poodle. Others claim that the mere fact that the Curly-Coated Retriever is the only breed named for its curly coat is an indication that this was the first of all of the curly-coated breeds. Unfortunately, since the hunters and breeders of the mid-1800s did not document their breeding practices or maintain breeding ledgers, there is no written record of breedings or of the people who

CANIS LUPUS

"Grandma, what big teeth you have!" The gray wolf, a familiar figure in fairy tales and legends, has had its reputation tarnished and its population pummeled over the centuries. Yet it is the descendants of this much-feared creature to which we open our homes and hearts. Our beloved dog, *Canis domesticus*, derives directly from the gray wolf, a highly social canine that lives in elaborately structured packs. In the wild, the gray wolf can range from 60 to 175 pounds, standing between 25 and 40 inches in height.

were involved in the development of today's Curly to prove any of these theories.

The early Curly-Coated Retriever was frequently referred to as a "meat dog," a generic term referring to a dog that would find and retrieve the birds regardless of hunting conditions or the gentility of his hunting master. Such was his nose and tenacity that the Curly was often used to find and retrieve birds left in a field already covered by "other breeds" during a driven shoot. Such a dog was an invaluable aid to the common man who hunted birds in order to provide meat for his family's dinner table.

In 1837, Thomas Bell wrote of the Curly in the *British Quadrupeds*: "The peculiar qualities and propensities of this dog, its exquisite sense of smell, its sagacity, strength and aquatic habits, have rendered it a most useful and important servant to a particular class of persons of the North of England and Scotland who live principally by shooting waterfowl, in the retrieving of which these dogs exhibit the highest degree of docility and hardihood." These remarks seem to validate the "meat-dog" Curly and the class of people most inclined to own and utilize the dog for bird work in water and afield.

Despite his murky history, there is definite proof that the Curly-Coated Retriever was the

first breed to be classified by The Kennel Club of England as a retriever and was the first retriever to be exhibited in England as a show dog, the latter occurring in 1860. Four years later, The Kennel Club split retrievers into two classes, Retrievers—Curly-Coated and Retrievers—Wavy Coated, offering the Curly official recognition as its own breed. The Curly continued to be shown on the bench but, by the late 1800s, the Labrador Retriever and the Flat-Coated Retriever far outnumbered the Curly-Coat at the shows. The Curly's popularity waned as the public showed a decided preference for the other retriever breeds.

As happened with most other large breeds, the two World Wars decimated breed numbers and in 1919 only five Curlies were

The Portuguese Water Dog derives from the same stock as most of the water-dog breeds.

ORIGINAL RETRIEVER
The Curly-Coated Retriever is considered to be the oldest of all of the retriever breeds.

registered with England's Kennel Club. The road back was long and slow, and after a brief surge in popularity during the late 1930s, numbers plummeted again, with only 13 registered in 1942 and 1943. The next few years were still lean, but a bit more promising, with 90 Curly registrations by 1947.

As there were so few Curly breeders during the early 1900s, the few predominant kennel prefixes of that time can be found in most modern Curly pedigrees if they were to be traced back many generations. Names most commonly known were those of Preston, Penworthan, Knysna, Notlaw and Coombehurst.

By the early 1930s, the Darelyn and Snaphill Curly kennels were producing noteworthy Curlies, but their progress was interrupted by World War II. Darelyn, however, was revived during the 1940s with their foundation stock, Delilah of Darelyn and Dru of Darelyn. Their progeny continued into the 1950s, along with that of the Akrow kennels, who gave us the important Turkamann and Sorona stock during that decade.

The Curly finally gained real prominence during the 1950s and 1960s, and breeders in Australia, New Zealand and the United States began to import Curly breeding stock from England. Darelyn Aristocrat, Irishit Straight Line and Prince of Knocksginan were imported into Australia to greatly influence the breed in that country.

In England, several other new kennels joined Darelyn in active breeding. Harkaway, Grinkle, Banworth, Burtoncurl, Siccawei, Renniston and Charcol all became important in the establishment of the breed as the Curly entered the second half of the 20th century.

Through the 1970s and 1980s, facing the growing popularity of the Labrador and Flat-Coated Retrievers, the Curly's numbers continued to grow at a slow but steady rate. In historic moments for the breed, during the 1980s Ch. Darelyn Rifleman earned Best in Show wins over entries of 16,315 and 23,627 at England's largest dog shows. Not surprisingly, he became a dominant producer of important Curlies in England, Australia, the United States and continental Europe. Rifleman and his progeny can be found today in almost every Curly pedigree throughout those countries.

THE CURLY IN AUSTRALIA AND NEW ZEALAND

For over a century, Australians have prized the Curly-Coated Retriever as a brave, intelligent and agile hunting dog. The sturdy Curly is often used to retrieve waterfowl as large as swans. Curlies have also been known to hunt Australian kangaroo, a feat that requires great courage as well as speed and natural hunting ability.

Most of the Curlies in Australia and New Zealand today date back to the breeding of native Curlies to English imports. The very important dog, NZ and GFTCh. Dual Ch. Waitoki Tamatakapua, who is behind many modern Australian and New

Hailing from the breed's homeland, Eng. Ch. Gladrags Jackaranda is an excellent representative of what judges seek in the show ring for the Curly-Coated Retriever. In the UK, a Curly must win in both the field and the show ring to earn a full championship.

Zealand bloodlines, was the product of a New Zealand field-trial champion and an English import bitch. Another significant pairing was that of English import Nelson Prince and his Australian-born daughter, Nelson Beauty. This breeding produced the important Australian Curly, Black Prince. Australian breeder Olaf Michelson of Victoria and his imported Tablik Curlies were the foundation of many of the country's home-bred Curly-Coated Retrievers.

During the 1950s and 1960s, Australian breeders imported Darelyn Aristocrat from England, along with Sarona Simon, Banworth Simon, Banworth Athene and Pegasus, dogs who are

THE COMMONER'S CURLY

The Curly in its native England was originally known as the commoner's, or "blue-collar," dog, because the breed was more often owned by English gamekeepers or poachers than by the gentry or wealthy aristocrats.

behind over three-quarters of modern Curly bloodlines. The accomplished New Zealand

PURE-BRED PURPOSE
Given the vast range of the world's 400 or so pure breeds of dog, it's fair to say that domestic dogs are the most versatile animal in the kingdom. From the tiny 1-pound lap dog to the 200-pound guard dog, dogs have adapted to every need and whim of their human masters. Humans have selectively bred dogs to alter physical attributes like size, color, leg length, mass and skull diameter in order to suit our own needs and fancies. Dogs serve humans not only as companions and guardians but also as hunters, exterminators, shepherds, rescuers, messengers, warriors, babysitters and more!

import, Ch. Waitoki Tuhora, QC, is also behind many of Australia's Curlies.

As word of the Curly-Coated Retriever spread across the Atlantic to North America, Australia began to export dogs to the United States and Canada, as well as to Germany, New Guinea and New Zealand, creating legions of new breed fanciers on other continents.

In New Zealand the Curly-Coated Retriever reigns, as the breed is the most popular hunting dog in that country. The Curly's intelligence, superb hunting ability and natural affinity for water earn the breed high marks with hunting enthusiasts and field-trial aficionados.

An unusual aspect of the Australian Curly is a smaller-sized variety that is well known in some parts of Australia, with some specimens much smaller than the Curly-Coated Retriever descibed in breed standards. This smaller version is a very popular duck dog, found mostly along the Murray River, where it is not surprisingly called the "Murray River Curly." The River Curlies are unregistered, and many River Curly fans feel it should be considered a separate breed.

THE CURLY IN THE UNITED STATES
Although America saw its first Curly-Coated Retriever in 1907, the

breed was not registered in the United States until 1924. Curly fanciers then were most enthusiastic about the breed's potential as a hunting dog; indeed, the breed prospered during the 1920s and 1930s, when Curlies were popular as both family pets and as gundogs. As in the UK, World War II impacted the breed almost to the point of total extinction, with only 16 specimens registered between 1941 and 1949. By 1950, when breeders of all breeds of dog were trying to re-establish their lines, the Labrador and Flat-Coated Retrievers had made huge inroads into the hunting populace, and many kennels began to produce faster and more stylish retrievers. Additionally, a rumor circulated in American dog circles that the Curly was hard-mouthed and that the breed's curly coat was difficult to maintain. Such false allegations led to a disastrous drop in Curly interest and support, reducing breed numbers to only two dogs registered in 1964. With a total lack of breeding stock, any remaining lines of Curly breeding stock were lost, and for a brief while the future of the breed looked bleak.

The breed's revival came in 1964, when Mr. Dale Dettweiler imported Eng. Ch. Siccawei Black Rod from England. This dog was affectionately called "Limey" by those who judged him in the show ring. Limey also worked in the

field and had quite a loyal following of hunters who spent many successful hours hunting behind the dog. After this most successful import, Mr. Dettweiler brought over more Curlies from England, Australia and New Zealand, and with those dogs he established his Curly kennel, bearing the prefix Windpatch. The Windpatch Curlies became the

Ch. Hie-On Mack MacLaig, the top-winning Curly of the late 1970s and early 1980s, is shown here with handler John Horan.

CURLIES IN AUSTRALIA

Breed history indicates presence of the Curly in Australia in the early 1800s. In 1897, Walter Bielby writes in *Dogs of Australia* about a Curly-Coated Retriever named Martins Ravensdown Ben at a turn-of-the-century dog show in Victoria.

Ch. Karakul Titan was a BIS winner and a top-ranked Curly in the late 1980s and early 1990s. Bred by Sheila Anderson and owned by John Mello.

The first all-breed-BIS-winning Curly in the US was Ch. Summerwind's Charles Dickens. Bred by Doris Hodges and owned by Sue Tokolics.

foundation for the breed in the United States, and Mr. Dettweiler is considered by many to be the savior of the modern American Curly.

During the 1970s, many of the owners and breeders who would shape the breed for the next 10 to 20 years obtained their first Curlies. This decade saw the start of Wit's End, Karakul, Sevenravens, Summerwind, Charwin, Mayhem, Nightflight, Lakeview, Jollybodies, Sandbar, Back Bay, Solimar and Ptarmigan, among others. Dogs including Limey, Conference Table, Lizah Nero and Carnsford Kyeema Patch, along with their progeny, became the foundation of these kennels. Also figuring into the pedigrees of Curlies owned by most of these

kennels in the 1970s was Ch. Windpatch Raven O'Goldendeed, Windpatch Devil O'Goldendeed and Windpatch Baron O'Goldendeed. These brothers were sired by Ch. Siccawei Black Rod out of Ch. Windpatch Nero's Lollipop.

The year 1966 saw the first supported Curly entry at the International Kennel Club benched show in Chicago. For the next 13 years, Curly owners met annually in Chicago for the only supported entry for the breed. In 1979, during the supported entry weekend, the Curly-Coated Retriever Club of America (CCRCA) was founded. There were 47 charter members, of which 10 are still active members of the club. Today there are over 200 members of the CCRCA, which was licensed by the American Kennel Club (AKC) in 1994.

The 1980s saw the birth of Aarowag, Jar-em, Coventry, El Mack, Mathel and Ranah, and the continuance of the breeding programs of Summerwind,

Mayhem, Charwin, Ptarmigan, Karakul, Jollybodies, Sandbar, Sevenravens and Wit's End. Curlies from these kennels who began to make a mark on the pedigrees of this decade were Banworth Ivurried, imported from England by Ptarmigan kennels; Ch. Windpatch Ebony Walkabout; Ch. Windpatch Demure Anne; Ch. Karakul Corona De Sombra; Ch. Sevenravens Windbell; Ch. Summerwind Echo's of Freedom and Ch. Charwin Scirocco, among others.

Mayhem kennel's Hie-on Mack MacLaig became the first Curly-Coated Retriever since Limey to have an outstanding show career. Although his show career was short, he was a Curly to remember and his records stood until 1996. In 1989, the first Curly to win an all-breed Best in Show (BIS) was Ch. Summerwind's Charles Dickens, bred by Doris Hodges and owned by Sue Tokolics.

The 1990s saw a real growth in the number of Curlies in this country and many new breeding kennels began to emerge. Some of the most successful are Avanti, Pizzazz, Riverwatch, Fairway, Addidas, Boyerie, Softmaple and Kurly Kreek. Two more Curlies won Best in Show awards; the first was Ch. Karakul Titan, bred by Sheila Anderson and owned by John Mello, in 1995. Titan was owner-handled to this win. Then in 1996 Ch. Mayhem's Gentlemen's

Agreement, bred by Mary Alice Hembrey and owned by Jane Anderson, captured a BIS. He did it again in 1997 to become the first Curly-Coated Retriever to win multiple Bests in Show. Baron was also owner-handled to his wins.

Eventually Curlies could be seen competing at shows across the country. As the year 2000 approached, Curly entries could be found in almost any part of the US. For the first time, Curlies began to be competitive in the Sporting Group. Ch. Ptarmigan Gale At Riverwatch, bred by Janean Marti and owned by Gary and Mary Meek, broke all of the American Curly records except BIS. She was the top-winning Curly for most of the 1990s, garnered five national specialty Best of Breed wins and won the breed at the prestigious Westminster Kennel Club show seven times. Always owner-handled, she was instrumental in

Ch. Ptarmigan Gale at Riverwatch ("Tempest") was the foundation of Riverwatch kennels and held many records in the breed with her multiple specialty, Sporting Group and Westminster wins. Bred by Janean Marti and owned by Gary and Mary Meek.

MBIS, MBISS, SR Ch. Fairway It's My Party, CGC, WCX, JH, bred by Kim Kiernan and owned by Susan Chow, enjoyed an extraordinary show career. "Rebel" had a most impressive Best in Show win over an entry of 2,500 dogs!

line that is beginning to be seen in pedigrees across the country. Charwin, Aarowag, Ptarmigan, Summerwind, Softmaple, Riverwatch, Kurly Kreek and Boyerie kennels are still active, with representatives of their breeding also included in many pedigrees. Ch. Mathel Felicitation, owned by Kim Kiernan of Fairway kennels, produced very well and her offspring are seen in many of our pedigrees and are also doing well in the show ring. Ch. Fairway It's My Party, bred by Kim Kiernan and owned by Susan Chow, had a sensational show career. Professional handler Mary Dukes piloted him to a record-breaking career that included four Bests in Show.

In 2001 Ch. Ptarmigan Groovin, bred and owned by Janean Marti, garnered a BIS in very limited showing. In 2002 Ch. Kurly Kreek Marshall Dillon Boyerie, bred by Scott and Kathy Shifflet and owned by Yvonne Cooper, won his Best in Show to cap off a very successful show career. Dillon's sister, Ch. Kurly Kreek Mae West, also had a very successful show career as has Ch. Kurly Kreek Stocking Stuffer.

making the Curly a true competitor at the Group and BIS levels in the United States. Other Curlies that made their mark during the 1990s in the show ring were BIS Ch. Karakul Titan, BIS Ch. Mayhem's Gentlemen's Agreement, Ch. Karakul Trademark, Ch. Boyerie's Andouille O' Wits End, BIS Ch. Kurly Kreek Marshall Dillon Boyerie, Ch. Kurly Kreek Mae West, Ch. Addidas Christmas Party and Ch. Addidas Alpha Monopoly.

As we entered the new millennium, the number of breeders producing Curlies also began to increase. Avanti and Pizzazz kennels are working together to produce some very lovely Curlies in California. They are producing a

Some of the newer breeders and their successful Curlies are the Dese kennels of Donald and Sonia Evans, whose Dese's Black As Coal was one of the dogs to beat in the early 2000s; the Shadowbrook kennels of Delene and Henry Vota, whose Ch. Shadowbrooks First PJ Party has enjoyed several years of being ranked in the top five Curlies and the Gladrags USA kennels of Rita Nelson, who is having success with Ch. Gladrags Phorse Be With You.

From the more established kennels we have Ch. Pizzazz Avanti Gonna Go Far, Riverwatch Windwalker, Ch. Fairway's Devilish Ace, Ch. Addidas General Sherman, Ch. Sundevil Cerulean, Ch. KyterCurl IDo What ILike, Ch. Jangio's Lightning Bug, Ch. Fairways Softmaple Finnheir and Ch. Riverwatch Quietly Makin Noiz, all in the top ten during the first five years of the new millennium.

The current top show Curly is BIS Ch. Riverwatch Southern Cross, bred and owned by Gary and Mary Meek and co-owned by Conrad and Ann Clippert. He has

three AKC and one United Kennel Club (UKC) Bests in Show (breeder-owner handled), a national specialty Best of Breed and a Westminster Best of Breed and was the number-one Curly-Coated Retriever for 2004 and 2005. He is the grandson of Ch. Ptarmigan Gale At Riverwatch, who still holds the all-time top-winning Curly bitch record.

Besides making their marks in the show ring, Curlies here in the United States are titling in field trials, obedience, agility, rally obedience and more, and they are still the favorite hunting companion of many. The breed continues to gain more supporters all the time. Although Curlies are now easier to come by than they were in the 1990s, the breed is still ranked near the bottom when it comes to litters produced in a year.

Winning Best of Breed at Westminster in 2002 is Ch. Kurly Kreek Marshall Dillon Boyerie, handled by Amy Walker under judge James Covey. Bred by Scott and Kathy Shifflet; owned by Yvonne Cooper.

Grandson of the famous Tempest, multiple-BIS winner Ch. Riverwatch Southern Cross ("Curlew") has made quite a name for himself as well, being number-one in the breed for 2004 and 2005.

Ch. Riverwatch Desert Wind is no fair-weather friend—the versatile Curly can do it all!

CHARACTERISTICS OF THE
CURLY-COATED RETRIEVER

PERSONALITY AND TEMPERAMENT

"Unique" may be the word to best describe the Curly-Coated Retriever. His tightly curled, water-repellent coat is his most distinguishing characteristic and the one that most often generates questions and conversation. However, the dog beneath the coat is equally unique in temperament and ability. The Curly is a highly intelligent and independent retriever, considered by many to be the most intelligent, but also the most willful, of all retriever breeds. Although (and because) they learn quickly, they also become bored very easily, which creates a training conundrum for the average owner or trainer who often tends to use repetitive techniques when training for simple obedience or everyday field work.

Despite the breed's seemingly hard-nosed qualities, the Curly's temperament is rather soft and yielding, and dominant or heavy-handed training approaches are rarely necessary. The Curly has a higher-than-average energy level and is more inquisitive than most other retrievers—two qualities that, combined, make for a very active dog in body and mind.

The Curly is a most loyal and gentle dog who makes an excellent family companion as well as a very capable gundog. Curlies are seldom aggressive with other dogs or animals. Adult Curlies are very gentle with youngsters, but because of their large size and great exuberance, they can sometimes be unintentionally rough in play and accidentally knock over small children. As with any other breed, Curlies should be supervised when playing or interacting with children.

The Curly-Coated Retriever is a fun-loving, water-loving, sporting dog, always ready to get his paws wet.

Given their strong social tendencies, Curlies do not thrive in isolation or as yard or kennel dogs; rather, they do best when living as integral parts of family units. As family members, they are independent and discerning, perhaps sometimes appearing aloof and undemonstrative, especially with strangers. Nonetheless, the Curly is gentle to all and is affectionate to those close to him. Because of his active nature, a Curly kept indoors should be well socialized and taught household manners from a very early age to help ensure his growth into a well-behaved canine citizen. Puppy socialization class, progressing to basic obedience training, is necessary if you hope to live in harmony with your Curly.

The Curly has an excellent memory and a great capacity for learning, which makes training both fun and challenging. Another important fact that affects their

Only the facial hair is short and smooth; the rest of a Curly-Coat's body is covered with small, tight curls.

> **WOOF!**
> The Curly is a discriminating barker who will bark at new or strange people or objects, but will not bark on endlessly. Intensely loyal to his family and loved ones, he is a good watchdog, but the Curly is not considered a protection breed.

training is that Curlies are known to be slower to mature than other retriever breeds. Thus, training sessions should be kept short, fun and interesting if you are to achieve long-term success in molding adult behavior. The breed's slow rate of maturity is a major factor in the working Curly, as few field trialers or professional trainers are interested in working with a dog who doesn't get serious about his work until he is three or four years old.

Curly-Coated Retrievers are known to be clever and creative in their quest for mischief or adventure. They require vigorous daily exercise to keep physically healthy and emotionally content. A yard with a six-foot fence is best for safe containment, as Curlies are quite adept at scaling lower fences. Also, while they are not known to be diggers, they will dig if bored and can dig under fences. They are not road- or traffic-wise, so would be at great risk of becoming injured or lost if roaming freely about the neighborhood.

PHYSICAL CHARACTERISTICS

Physically, the Curly is a large dog of sturdy structure who can weigh anywhere from 50 to 100 pounds; the average is between 65 to 80 pounds, with males on the larger end of the spectrum. His very curly coat is his most unusual characteristic, composed of very small, hard, tight, waterproof curls that extend from the back of the head down to the elbows and hocks to the tip of the tail, with only the face devoid of any curls. Only his short facial hair grows straight and smooth. Curlies come in either black or liver, with black being the more predominant color.

The Curly's coat is virtually briar- and bramble-proof, and in most cases the hard tight curls will not allow burrs or seeds to penetrate, a feature that is prized by hunters who work with the breed. In water, the coat is equally efficient, offering far better protection than the coats of his other retriever relatives. Hunters claim that, of all of the retriever breeds, the Curly's coat offers the most ideal insulation and protection, keeping his skin warm and dry during a full day's shoot, which is especially important when hunting in bleak, icy, winter conditions.

The distinctive coat is easy for the owner to maintain. It does not require daily care, nor should it be brushed or combed, as this would be detrimental to the tight curls. Only during the spring and fall shedding periods does the coat need to be brushed. Shedding is not a problem with this breed, as throughout the rest of the year only slight routine shedding occurs.

Bathing is necessary three or four times a year, as the coat tends to get oily and gather dust and debris. For the allergic Curly owner, bathing the dog will get rid of potential irritants that have gathered in the coat. For working Curlies, even less frequent bathing is necessary. Swimming serves the same function as bathing in that the water removes dirt and dust from the coat. However, any Curly used for water or field work should be checked often to ensure that no burrs, insects, etc., have taken up residence in the coat, in the ears or anywhere else on the body.

ENERGY AND ABILITY

Like his American descendant, the Chesapeake Bay Retriever, the Curly is exceptionally powerful for his size. Although not as fast or stylish as the Labrador or

SHEDDING CYCLE

Intact female Curlies shed their coats just before every heat cycle. The coat will grow back within six to eight weeks after shedding.

MASTERS OF ESCAPE
Curlies are known to be masterful escape artists and, if left unsupervised, will figure out how to escape from most fenced enclosures.

feels ready to do so. He will soon gain confidence and be splashing about on his own.

Because he is a large-breed dog with a high energy level, a Curly-Coated Retriever needs a securely fenced yard and an active family who will give its dog lots of daily exercise. A Curly will be happier and safer being active with you rather than left in the fenced yard on his own to amuse himself. With a Curly puppy, though, jumping and high-impact exercise should be avoided before one year of age to avoid stress on growing joints.

Curly owners have the opportunity to participate in a wide range of activities with their dogs. The Curly-Coated Retriever loves to take part in activities that allow him to expend some energy. It is even better if the activity allows him to make use of his instinctive abilities.

The Curly today still excels at the task for which he was intended—that of finding and retrieving game birds, both in water and on land. Hunters who work with their Curlies find the dogs to be tremendous assets, and many Curlies participate in organized field-trial competition.

Aside from field work and trials, other popular activities for the Curly include hunting tests, obedience competition, agility trials and flyball. The most important key to success in training

Golden Retriever, he nevertheless has tremendous endurance, working at a steady, sensible pace and never seeming to tire. Many hunters claim that the Curly's most remarkable quality is his perseverance; he just will not give up on a bird.

Curlies are exceptionally good swimmers, and they love to swim! Most will dive enthusiastically into any body of water at every opportunity. However, one should still exercise caution when introducing a puppy to water. Never throw or push a pup into the water; always allow him to approach and enter it when he your Curly for anything is to build a foundation when the puppy is quite young. This will provide the best start to your future together. Since that cute Curly puppy will mature into a large and rather willful dog, the owner is wise to teach him basic obedience commands early on so he will grow into a responsive and well-behaved companion.

HEREDITARY HEALTH CONCERNS

Nearly every breed of dog is plagued by certain hereditary diseases, some of which are common to several types or groups of dogs. For example, cancers are on the rise in the Curly, and seizures are found to some degree; however, these problems also are common to many of today's dog breeds. Other health problems are more breed-specific. Regardless, there are a few health problems of which every Curly owner or prospective owner should be aware. While the majority of Curly-Coated Retrievers will not be affected by health problems, owners who are informed of potential problems will be better able to notice the signs and provide their dogs with prompt veterinary care.

PATTERNED BALDNESS
The most widespread health problem in the Curly-Coated Retriever is patterned baldness. This

GENE DROOL
Curlies are known to drool at times, a trait that may stem from their Newfoundland relatives.

usually manifests itself in bilateral hair loss, meaning on both sides of the dog, with bald strips or patches appearing on the backs of the rear legs, on the neck, on the throat and behind the shoulders. Thin, brittle and uncurled hair is another common symptom. In mild cases, the patterning may appear only once and never again appear after the hair grows back. However, it is a symptom of a greater problem, as it is caused by an auto-immune deficiency. Affected dogs are more likely to have allergies, reproductive problems and growth-hormone prob-

Because the Curly is single-coated, he sheds much less than retriever breeds that have double coats.

Like most other
gundogs, the
Curly-Coat is a
gregarious,
friendly soul, able
to get along with
most other dogs.
This senior Curly
is sharing a walk
with a young
German Wire-
haired Pointer.

Like most other gundogs, the Curly-Coat is a gregarious, friendly soul, able to get along with most other dogs. This senior Curly is sharing a walk with a young German Wire-haired Pointer.

lems wherein the dog matures to only about 40 pounds.

An affected dog may have a good coat as a puppy, with bald spots developing when the dog reaches sexual maturity. Seemingly unaffected adults can produce patterned pups, so it is important for the breeder to know the genetics behind any dogs being used for breeding purposes.

Patterned baldness is easily and frequently misdiagnosed. Many veterinarians are unfamiliar with this particular problem and can easily blame the bald spots on diet deficiency or wear from a too-wide collar. Unfortunately, special diets and supplements do not help patterned baldness.

Although the condition is not life-threatening, and mildly affected Curlies will live normal, healthy lives, dogs affected to any degree should not be bred.

HIP DYSPLASIA (HD)

Hip dysplasia means, quite simply, poor or abnormal formation of the hip joint. HD most commonly occurs in large breeds of dog and is known to be inherited. A severe case can render a hunting dog worthless in the field, and even a mild case can cause painful arthritic changes in the average house dog. Less severe cases may go undetected until changes in the dog's mobility indicate a problem.

HD is caused by several recessive genes, which unfortunately means that dogs with cleared (non-dysplastic) hips could carry dysplastic genes that may pass on to their progeny. HD can be diagnosed only through x-ray examination, and only by screening several generations of breeding stock can a breeder be better assured of offspring with healthy hips.

While hip dysplasia is largely an inherited condition, research shows that environmental factors also play a significant part in its development. Overfeeding and feeding a diet high in calories (primarily fat) during a puppy's rapid-growth stages are suspected to be contributing factors in the development of HD. Heavy-bodied and overweight puppies are more at risk than pups with lean conformation.

Dogs 24 months of age and older should have their hips x-rayed and the x-rays evaluated to determine if any degree of dysplasia is present. X-rays should be submitted to the Orthopedic Foundation for Animals (OFA) for evaluation and grading by a panel of certified veterinary radiologists. There are seven possible grades: Excellent, Good, Fair, Borderline, Mild,

HEART-HEALTHY

In this modern age of ever-improving cardio-care, no doctor or scientist can dispute the advantages of owning a dog to lower a person's risk of heart disease. Studies have proven that petting a dog, walking a dog and grooming a dog all show positive results toward lowering your blood pressure. The simple routine of exercising your dog—going outside with the dog and walking, jogging or playing catch—is heart-healthy in and of itself. If you are normally less active than your physician thinks you should be, adopting a dog may be a smart option to improve your own quality of life as well as that of another creature.

To work, to play and to run, as all Curlies love to do, a dog must have healthy, strong hips and elbows.

several problems, including ununited anconeal process, fragmented coronoid process and osteochondritis dissecans. ED can be detected only through x-ray; a testing and grading program similar to that used for hip dysplasia is offered by the OFA. Ask the breeder if he has had ED testing done on his breeding stock, as many do.

EYE PROBLEMS
There are many types of heredi-tary eye disease that affect dogs. Eye problems are not too common in the Curly but have been cited, among them ectropion and entropion (eyelid abnormalities), distichiasis (eyelash abnormality), several types of cataracts, persistent pupillary membrane and dysplasia of the cornea and/or the retina. While some of these problems are easily fixed, others can lead to vision problems at some stage of a dog's life. For example, some cataracts do not interfere with a dog's vision, but others can progress into partial or complete blindness. Fortunately, surgery is now available to treat

Moderate and Severe. Dogs whose hips are graded Excellent, Good and Fair will receive OFA numbers. The other four gradings do not warrant an OFA number, with the latter three indicating that the dog is affected by some level of dysplasia. Dogs that do not receive OFA numbers should not be used in breeding programs.

Anyone looking for a healthy Curly puppy should make certain that the sire and dam of any litter under consideration have their certificates of clearance from the OFA or another accredited organi-zation; similar hip-testing programs are in place in countries around the world. Good breeders have all of their breeding stock tested and only breed from those dogs and bitches who have received appropriate clearances.

ELBOW DYSPLASIA (ED)
Like HD, elbow dysplasia is a developmental joint disease; ED affects the elbow. It involves

> **DON'T WANNA GROW UP!**
> The Curly-Coat is considered a slow-maturing breed. Curlies are puppy-like until at least two years old, reaching physical and emotional maturity at about three-and-a-half years of age.

DO YOU KNOW ABOUT HIP DYSPLASIA?

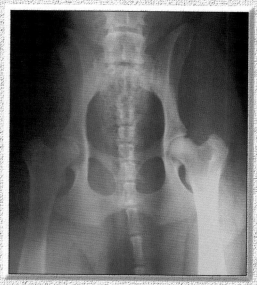

X-ray of a dog with "Good" hips.

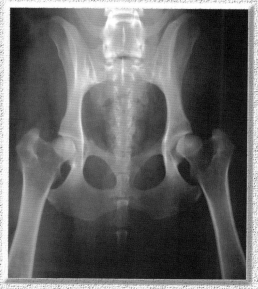

X-ray of a dog with "Moderate" dysplastic hips.

Hip dysplasia is a fairly common condition found in pure-bred dogs. When a dog has hip dysplasia, his hind leg has an incorrectly formed hip joint. By constant use of the hip joint, it becomes more and more loose, wears abnormally and may become arthritic.

Hip dysplasia can only be confirmed with an x-ray, but certain symptoms may indicate a problem. Your dog may have a hip dysplasia problem if he walks in a peculiar manner, hops instead of smoothly runs, uses his hind legs in unison (to keep the pressure off the weak joint), has trouble getting up from a prone position or always sits with both legs together on one side of his body.

As the dog matures, he may adapt well to life with a bad hip, but in a few years the arthritis develops and many dogs with hip dysplasia become crippled.

Hip dysplasia is considered an inherited disease and only can be diagnosed definitively by x-ray when the dog is two years old, although symptoms often appear earlier. Some experts claim that a special diet might help your puppy outgrow the bad hip, but the usual treatments are surgical. The removal of the pectineus muscle, the removal of the round part of the femur, reconstructing the pelvis and replacing the hip with an artificial one are all surgical interventions that are expensive, but they are usually very successful. Follow the advice of your veterinarian.

many types of cataract with a high rate of success.

Progressive retinal atrophy (PRA) and retinal dysplasia (RD) are inherited defects of the retina (or light-receptor area of the eye). Unlike the progressive deterioration that occurs with PRA, RD does not result in total blindness; instead it will affect a working dog's ability to function at a chosen task. Dogs with either condition should be removed from breeding programs.

All eye problems can only be diagnosed by a veterinary ophthalmologist. As age of onset for the different problems varies widely, with some evident in puppyhood and some not appearing until later in life, annual eye exams and certification from the Canine Eye Registration Foundation (CERF) is very important. All Curlies should be cleared before breeding; affected animals should not be bred. Ask the breeder for current exam results and eye clearances on the parents of your puppy.

HEART PROBLEMS

Just as in humans, there are various types of heart problems that can affect dogs and the Curly-Coated Retriever is not immune. The OFA maintains databases for other types of hereditary disease beyond orthopedic problems; it also issues cardiac gradings based on examinations performed by certified veterinarians with specialties or advanced training in canine cardiology. The grading system is based on the absence or presence of heart murmurs and, if present, the severity. Presence of a heart murmur is often indicative of a problem and is the best way to rule out dogs for breeding as the modes of inheritance for some of the major heart diseases are yet unknown. While the OFA does not consider itself as a screening tool for these diseases, a dog should still receive an OFA cardiac clearance before being bred.

BLOAT, A DEADLY PROBLEM

Any dog can contract gastric torsion (more familiarly known as "bloat") but those that are large and deep-chested, including all of the retriever breeds, are at the greatest risk. Bloat is a condition in which the stomach fills with air and turns on itself, cutting off exit points and causing great pain to the dog, with shock and death following quickly. It is a very serious problem that requires immediate veterinary attention. There are daily precautions that you should incorporate into your dog's routine to protect your Curly-Coat. The condition and its symptoms, causes, preventives and treatment are discussed in more detail in the sections on feeding and exercise in the chapter on everyday care.

Discuss the occurrence
of eye problems with
your chosen breeder.
All breeding stock
should be screened for
potential problems,
and no visually
impaired dogs should
ever be bred.

The breed standard describes the ideal dog and is used by breeders as they plan their breedings and by judges as a "yardstick" to measure the quality of dogs competing in shows. Ch. Addidas Christmas Party was among the top show dogs in the breed in the 1990s.

CURLY-COATED RETRIEVER

To fully appreciate the elements of any breed standard, one must first understand why a standard is necessary in the first place. In order to preserve a breed's unique characteristics, the original breed specialists who formed the breed's parent club(s) adopted a standard, for without a detailed description to use as a guideline for future breedings, many of the breed's valued qualities could easily become weakened or lost completely. The Curly was developed over many decades by fanciers and hunters who prized this breed for those special qualities that best served their needs and desires, whether working in the water, retrieving in the field or spending time in the home. Therefore, the intent of the Curly standard is to preserve and promote the integrity of every aspect of the breed, physical and temperamental.

THE AKC STANDARD FOR THE CURLY-COATED RETRIEVER

General Appearance: This smartly upstanding, multi-purpose hunting retriever is recognized by most canine historians as one of the oldest of the retrieving breeds. Developed in England, the Curly was long a favorite of English gamekeepers. Prized for innate field ability, courage and indomitable perseverance, a correctly built and tempered Curly will work as long as there is work to be done, retrieving both fur and feather in the heaviest of cover and the iciest of waters. To work all day a Curly must be balanced and sound, strong and robust, and quick and agile. Outline, carriage and attitude all combine for a grace and elegance somewhat uncommon among the other retriever breeds, providing the unique, upstanding quality desired

Top conformation dog BIS Ch. Riverwatch Southern Cross embodies correct type for the Curly-Coated Retriever.

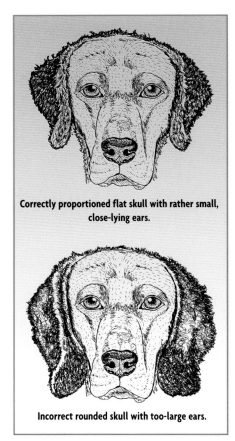

Correctly proportioned flat skull with rather small, close-lying ears.

Incorrect rounded skull with too-large ears.

The perfect coat is a dense mass of small, tight, distinct, crisp curls. The Curly is wickedly smart and highly trainable and, as such, is cherished as much for his role as loyal companion at home as he is in the field.

Size, Proportion, Substance: Ideal height at withers: dogs, 25 to 27 inches; bitches, 23 to 25 inches. A clearly superior Curly falling outside of this range should not be penalized because of size. The body proportions are slightly off square, meaning that the dog is slightly longer from prosternum to buttocks as he is from withers to ground. The Curly is both sturdy and elegant. The degree of substance is sufficient to ensure strength and endurance without sacrificing grace. Bone and substance are neither spindly nor massive and should be in proportion with weight and height and balanced throughout.

in the breed. In outline, the Curly is moderately angulated front and rear and, when comparing height to length, gives the impression of being higher on leg than the other retriever breeds. In carriage, the Curly is an erect, alert, self-confident dog. In motion, all parts blend into a smooth, powerful, harmonious symmetry. The coat, a hallmark of the breed, is of great importance for all Curlies, whether companion, hunting or show dogs.

Head: The head is a longer-than-wide wedge, readily distinguishable from that of all other retriever breeds and of a size in balance with the body. Length of foreface is equal, or nearly equal, to length of backskull and, when viewed in profile, the planes are parallel. The stop is shallow and sloping. At the point of joining, the width of foreface may be slightly less than the width of the backskull but blending of the two should be smooth. The head has a nearly straight, continuous taper to the nose and is clean cut, not coarse, blocky or cheeky. *Expression*—Intelligent and alert. *Eyes*—Almond-shaped, rather large but not too prominent. Black or brown in black dogs and brown or amber in liver dogs. Harsh yellow eyes and loose haws are undesirable. *Ears*—Rather small, set on a line slightly above the corner of the eye and lying close to the head. *Backskull*—Flat or nearly flat. *Foreface*—*Muzzle* is wedge-shaped with no hint of snipiness. The taper ends mildly, neither acutely pointed nor bluntly squared-off but rather slightly rounding at the bottom. Mouth is level and never wry. Jaws are long and strong. A scissors bite is preferred. Teeth set straight and even. The lips are tight and clean, not pendulous. The nose is fully pigmented; black on black dogs, brown on liver dogs. Nostrils are large.

Neck, Topline, Body: *Neck*—Strong and slightly arched, of medium length, free from throatiness and flowing freely into moderately laid-back shoulders. *Backline*—The back, that portion of the body from the rear point of the withers to the beginning of the loin, is strong and level. The loin, that part of the body extending from the end of the rib cage to the start of the pelvis, is short and muscular. The croup, that portion of the body from the start of the pelvis to the tail set-on, is only slightly sloping. *Body*—Chest is decidedly deep and not too wide, oval in cross-section, with brisket reaching elbow. While the impression of the chest should be of depth not width, the chest is not pinched or narrow. The ribs are well-sprung, neither barrel-shaped nor slab-sided, and extend well back into a deep, powerful loin with a moderate tuck-up of flank. *Tail*—

Correct level backline and rear, with hocks low to ground.   **Incorrect dip in backline, high in rear, weak hocks.**

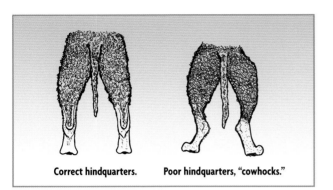

Correct hindquarters.   Poor hindquarters, "cowhocks."

Carried straight or fairly straight, never docked and reaching approximately to the hock. Never curled over the back and should not be kinked or crooked. Covered with curls and, if trimmed, tapering toward the point.

Forequarters: Shoulder blades are very long, well covered with muscle, and are moderately laid back at about a 55 degree angle. The width between shoulder blades is adequate to allow enough flexibility to easily retrieve game. Upper arm bones are about equal in length with shoulder blades and laid back at approximately the same angle as the blades, meaning the forelegs are set under the withers. The equal length of shoulder blade and upper arm bone and the balanced angulation between the two allows for good extension of the front legs. The forelegs are straight with strong, true pasterns. Feet are round and compact, with well-arched toes and thick pads. Front dewclaws are generally removed.

Hindquarters: Strong and in balance with front angulation. Thighs are powerful with muscling carrying well down into the second thigh. Stifle is of moderate bend. The hocks are strong and true, turning neither in nor out, with hock joint well let down. Rear dewclaws are generally removed.

Coat: The coat is a distinguishing characteristic and quite different from that of any other breed. The body coat is a thick mass of small, tight, crisp curls, lying close to the skin, resilient, water resistant and of sufficient density to provide protection against weather, water and punishing cover. Curls also extend up the entire neck to the occiput, down the thigh and back leg to at least the hock and over the entire tail. Elsewhere, the coat is short, smooth and straight, including on the forehead, face, front of forelegs and feet. A patch of uncurled hair behind the withers or bald patches anywhere on the body, including bald strips down the back of the legs or a triangular bald patch on the throat, should be severely penalized. A looser, more open curl is acceptable on the ears. Sparse, silky, fuzzy or very harsh, dry or brittle hair is a fault. *Trimming*—Feathering may be trimmed from the ears, belly, backs of forelegs, thighs, pasterns, hocks and feet. On the tail, feathering should be removed. Short trimming of the coat on the ear is permitted but shearing of the body coat is undesirable.

Color: Black or liver. Either color is correct. A prominent white patch is undesirable but a few white hairs are allowable in an otherwise good dog.

Gait: The dual function of the Curly as both waterfowl retriever and upland game hunter demands a dog who moves with strength and power yet is quick and agile. The ground-covering stride is a well-coordinated melding of grace and power, neither mincing nor lumbering. The seemingly effortless trot is efficient and balanced front to rear. When viewed from the side, the reach in front and rear is free-flowing, not stilted or hackneyed. When viewed from the front or rear, movement is true: the front legs turn neither in nor out and the rear legs do not cross. Well-developed, muscular thighs and strong hocks do their full share of work, contributing to rear thrust and drive. The extension in front is strong and smooth and in balance with rear action. Balance in structure translates to balance in movement and is of great importance to ensure soundness and endurance; extremes of angulation and gait are not desirable.

Temperament: Self-confident, steadfast and proud, this active, intelligent dog is a charming and gentle family companion and a determined, durable hunter. The Curly is alert, biddable and responsive to family and friends, whether at home or in the field. Of independent nature and discerning intelligence, a Curly sometimes appears aloof or self-willed, and, as such, is often less demonstrative, particularly toward strangers, than the other retriever breeds. The Curly's independence and poise should not be confused with shyness or a lack of willingness to please. In the show ring, a correctly-tempered Curly will steadily stand his ground, submit easily to examination and might or might not wag his tail when doing so. In the field, the Curly is eager, persistent and inherently courageous. At home, he is calm and affectionate. Shyness is a fault and any dog who shies away from show ring examination should be penalized. Minor allowances can be made for puppies who misbehave in the show ring due to overexuberance or lack of training or experience.

Approved October 12, 1993
Effective November 30, 1993

The word "puppy" defines the Curly for the first few years of life...are you up to the challenge? If so, you will reap the rewards of everything this one-of-a-kind breed has to offer.

CURLY-COATED RETRIEVER

FINDING A BREEDER

The puppy selection process for Curly-Coated Retrievers is quite the same as with most breeds of dog. A reputable breeder is the most reliable source for a quality pup who is healthy and will possess the qualities typical of the breed. Because the breed is numerically small in most countries, finding a good breeder may be a challenge, but a long and happy future with your puppy is worth the extra effort involved in seeking out a responsible puppy source. Veterinarians, breed and kennel clubs, dog shows and outdoor field events are all good sources of information about the breed and breeders. Start by contacting the Curly-Coated Retriever Club of America (www.ccrca.org), who can refer you to member breeders and give you information about events in which you can see Curlies in action and meet Curly people.

Once you have located a trustworthy breeder, both you and the breeder should have questions about each other. Your concern is the health and stability of the pups, and the breeder should be interested in you as a dog owner and what kind of home you will provide for the little one. If the breeder fails to make any inquiries about you and is willing to sell you a puppy without asking any questions, you would be wise to look elsewhere for a pup.

Breeders typically want to know where the dog will live, who will care for him, where and how the dog will exercise, what other pets you own or have owned, how many children are in the house, why you want a Curly-Coated Retriever and how much time you have to devote to the dog. The breeder should also discuss health and genetic problems within the breed, especially any in his own lines. No bloodline is problem-free; if the breeder

Meeting and interacting with the puppy is a basic requirement when selecting the right Curly for you.

A cozy bed and safe toys to chew will help the Curly pup settle into his new home.

makes such a claim, it is best to move on in your puppy search.

The breeder should be able to provide answers to the following questions:

• Do both parents have hip clearances from an accredited organization such as the OFA? A statement from a veterinarian is not a valid clearance.

• Have both parents been examined for hereditary eye disease and do they have current clearances from CERF (eyes should be retested annually)?

• Does the breeder have OFA cardiac clearances for the sire and dam?

• How often is the dam bred? If bred every heat cycle, this is too often and may indicate that profit is the breeder's primary motive.

• Is the breeder knowledgeable about the breed and is he involved in some element of competition or activity with his dogs? Does he belong to a breed or kennel club?

• Does the breeder have only one or two breeds of dog? Does he have only one, perhaps two litters at a time? If there are several breeds of dog, the breeder cannot devote sufficient time to becoming really knowledgeable about each breed. If there is more than one litter, it is equally difficult to give the pups the time and attention that they need.

• Is the breeder willing to provide you with references of other people who have purchased puppies from him?

• Does the breeder have a written contract, and does the contract include a breeding restriction with a mandatory spay/neuter provision for pet dogs?

• Does the breeder guarantee the health of this puppy, and for

MAKE A COMMITMENT
Dogs are most assuredly man's best friend, but they are also a lot of work. When you add a puppy to your family, you also are adding to your daily responsibilities for years to come. Dogs need more than just food, water and a place to sleep. They also require training (which is ongoing throughout the lifetime of the dog), activity to keep them physically and mentally fit and hands-on attention every day, plus grooming and health care. Your life as you now know it may well disappear! Are you prepared for such drastic changes?

how long, and will he take the pup back at any time for any reason if you cannot keep him? (This is the ultimate hallmark of responsible breeding.) Does the contract offer another puppy or money back in case of health or other problems with the puppy? Many unscrupulous breeders will honor guarantees only after the puppy is destroyed, asserting that they will never have to replace sick puppies.

• Why did the breeder plan this particular breeding between this sire and dam? "He (or she) is a very sweet dog" or similar evasive answers are not sufficient reasons to breed an animal.

• Can you meet the parents of the litter? The dam should most certainly be available and, if the sire is not, you should be able to view photos and paperwork on the sire.

• Will the breeder provide you with a copy of a three- to five-generation pedigree? Does the pedigree contain any titles before or after the dogs' names (e.g., Ch., OTCh, CD, JH, WC) in the first two generations? The term "championship lines" is meaningless if those titles are three or more generations back in any pedigree.

• Have the pups been raised in the home, not isolated in a kennel building or barn, and have they been socialized with other people, adults and children alike?

• Do the pups seem healthy, with no discharge from their eyes

SIGNS OF A HEALTHY PUPPY
Healthy puppies are robust little fellows who are alert and active, sporting shiny coats and supple skin. They should not appear lethargic, bloated or pot-bellied, nor should they have flaky skin or runny or crusted eyes or noses. Their stools should be firm and well formed, with no evidence of blood or mucus.

or noses, no loose stools, no foul-smelling ears? Are their coats healthy and clean? Do they appear energetic and playful when awake? Are they happy and confident around visitors, not cringing, timid or fearful?

• Have the pups been wormed, had their first shots, been checked by a veterinarian? Does the breeder provide copies of health records and health clearances as well as literature to help you with feeding, house-training and obedience training?

• Do you feel comfortable with the breeder? Do you feel pressured or intimidated? Can you ask him questions without feeling like you are stupid or imposing? Will he be available and willing to answer questions throughout the life of this dog?

SELECTING A PUPPY

You have contacted and met a breeder or two, you have made your choice about which breeder is best suited to your needs, you are armed with your list of questions and you are ready to visit the litter. Keep in mind that many top breeders have waiting lists. However, even if the pups are already "spoken for," these visits are invaluable educational experiences and you can then be put on the breeder's list for an available puppy from an upcoming litter.

Once a litter becomes available, you will have a good selection from which to choose; Curly litters average about six pups, some being as large as eight or nine. Since you are likely to be choosing a Curly as a pet dog and not a field or show dog, you simply should select a pup that is friendly, attractive and healthy. If you are selecting a Curly for hunting or field-trialing, you are well advised to buy the pup from a breeder whose dogs are accom-

MALE OR FEMALE?

Regarding gender differences, some males may be more dominant and stronger willed, but this is more dependent on the individual personality of each male or female. Males are larger, usually outweighing the females by 10 to 20 pounds.

plished in gundog activities. Always check the bite of your selected puppy to be sure that it is neither overshot nor undershot. This may not be too noticeable on a young puppy, but will become more evident as the puppy gets older.

Breeders commonly allow visitors to see their litters by around the fifth or sixth week, and puppies leave for their new homes between the eighth and tenth week. Breeders who permit their puppies to leave early are more interested in your money than in their puppies' well-being. Puppies need to learn the rules of the pack from their dams, and most dams continue teaching the pups manners and dos and don'ts until around the eighth week. Breeders spend significant amounts of time with the Curly toddlers so that the pups are able to interact with the "other species," i.e., humans. Given the long history that dogs and humans have, bonding between the two species is natural but must be nurtured. A well-bred, well-socialized Curly pup wants nothing more than to be near you and please you.

A COMMITTED NEW OWNER

By now you should understand what makes the Curly-Coated Retriever a most unique and special dog, one that may fit nicely into your family and lifestyle. If you have researched breeders, you

A SHOW PUPPY

If you plan to show your puppy, you must first deal with a reputable breeder who shows his dogs and has had some success in the conformation ring. The puppy's pedigree should include one or more champions in the first and second generation. You should be familiar with the breed and breed standard so you can know what qualities to look for in your puppy. The breeder's observations and recommendations also are invaluable aids in selecting your future champion. If you consider an older puppy, be sure that the puppy has been properly socialized with people and other animals, as he will have been with the breeder throughout his crucial socialization period.

The acquisition of any dog, particularly an intelligent and active breed like the Curly, requires the cooperation and consent of the whole family. Everyone must participate in the selection, care and training of the puppy.

PET INSURANCE

Just as you can insure your car, your house and your own health, you likewise can insure your dog's health. Investigate a pet insurance policy by talking to your vet. Depending on the age of your dog, the breed and the kind of coverage you desire, your policy can be very affordable. Most policies cover accidental injuries, poisoning and thousands of medical problems and illnesses, including cancers. Some carriers also offer routine care and immunization coverage.

should be able to recognize a knowledgeable and responsible Curly-Coated Retriever breeder who cares not only about his pups but also about what kind of owner you will be. If you have completed the final step in your new journey, you have found a litter, or possibly two, of quality Curly pups.

A visit with the puppies and their breeder should be an education in itself. Breed research, breeder selection and puppy visitation are very important aspects of finding the puppy of your dreams. Beyond that, these things also lay the foundation for a successful future with your pup. Puppy personalities within each litter vary, from the shy and easygoing puppy to the one who is dominant and assertive, with most pups falling somewhere in between. By spending time with the puppies you will be able to recognize certain behaviors and what these behaviors indicate about each pup's temperament. Which type of pup will complement your family dynamics is best determined by observing the puppies in action within their "pack." Your breeder's expertise and recommendations are also valuable. Although you may fall in love with a bold and brassy male, the breeder may suggest that another pup would be best for you. The breeder's experience in rearing Curly-Coated Retriever pups and matching their temperaments with appropriate humans offers the best assurance that your pup will meet your needs and expectations. The type of puppy that you select is just as important as your decision that the Curly is the breed for you.

The decision to live with a Curly-Coated Retriever is a serious commitment and not one to be taken lightly. This puppy is a living sentient being that will be dependent on you for basic survival for his entire life. Beyond the basics of survival—food, water, shelter and protection—he needs much, much more. The

PEDIGREE VS. REGISTRATION CERTIFICATE
Too often new owners are confused between these two important documents. Your puppy's pedigree, essentially a family tree, is a written record of a dog's genealogy of three generations or more. The pedigree will show you the names as well as performance titles of all dogs in your pup's background. Your breeder must provide you with a registration application, with his part properly filled out. You must complete the application and send it to the AKC with the proper fee. Every puppy must come from a litter that has been AKC-registered by the breeder, born in the US and from a sire and dam that are also registered with the AKC.

The seller must provide you with complete records to identify the puppy. The AKC requires that the seller provide the buyer with the following: breed; sex, color and markings; date of birth; litter number (when available); names and registration numbers of the parents; breeder's name; and date sold or delivered.

new pup needs love, nurturing and a proper canine education to mold him into a responsible, well-behaved canine citizen. Your Curly-Coated Retriever's health and good manners will need consistent monitoring and regular "tune-ups," so your job as a responsible dog owner will be ongoing throughout every stage of his life. If you are not prepared to accept these responsibilities and commit to them for at least the next decade, likely longer, then you are not prepared to own a dog of any breed.

NEW RELEASES

Most breeders release their puppies between eight to ten weeks of age. A breeder who allows puppies to leave the litter at five or six weeks of age is more concerned with profit than with the puppies' welfare. However, some breeders of show or working breeds may hold one or more top-quality puppies longer than ten weeks in order to evaluate the puppies' career or show potential and decide which one(s) they will keep for themselves.

Although the responsibilities of owning a dog may at times tax your patience, the joy of living with your Curly-Coated Retriever far outweighs the workload, and a well-mannered adult dog is worth your time and effort. Before your very eyes, your new charge will grow up to be your most loyal friend, devoted to you unconditionally.

YOUR CURLY-COATED RETRIEVER SHOPPING LIST

Just as expectant parents prepare a nursery for their baby, so should you ready your home for the arrival of your Curly-Coated Retriever pup. If you have the necessary puppy supplies purchased and in place before he comes home, it will ease the puppy's transition from the warmth and familiarity of his mom and littermates to the brand-new environment of his new home and human family. You will be too busy to stock up and prepare your house after your pup comes home, that's for sure! Imagine how a pup must feel upon being transported to a strange new place. It's up to you to comfort him and to let your little pup know that he is going to be happy with you!

FOOD AND WATER BOWLS

Your puppy will need separate bowls for his food and water. Stainless steel pans are generally preferred over plastic bowls since they sterilize better and pups are less inclined to chew on the metal. Heavy-duty ceramic bowls are popular, but consider how often you will have to pick up those heavy bowls! Buy adult-sized bowls, as your puppy will grow into them quickly.

THE DOG CRATE

If you think that crates are tools of punishment and confinement for when a dog has misbehaved, think again. Most breeders and almost all trainers recommend a crate as the preferred house-training aid as well as for all-around puppy training and safety. Because dogs are natural den creatures that prefer cave-like environments, the benefits of crate use are many. The crate provides the puppy with his very own "safe house," a cozy place to sleep, take a break or seek comfort with a favorite toy; a travel aid to house your dog when on the road,

Am./Can. Ch. Ptarmigan Gale at Riverwatch is the top Curly bitch in US history, but to these pups her most important achievement is being the number-one mom!

at motels or at the vet's office; a training aid to help teach your puppy proper toileting habits; a place of solitude when non-dog people happen to drop by and don't want a lively puppy—or even a well-behaved adult dog—saying hello or begging for attention.

Crates come in several types, although the wire crate and the fiberglass airline-type crate are the most popular. Both are safe and your puppy will adjust to either one, so the choice is up to you. The wire crates offer better visibility for the pup as well as better ventilation. Many of the wire crates easily fold into suitcase-size carriers. The fiberglass crates, similar to those used by the airlines for animal transport, are sturdier and more den-like. However, the fiberglass crates do not fold down and are less ventilated than wire crates; this can be problematic in hot weather. Some of the newer crates are made of

TEMPERAMENT ABOVE ALL ELSE

Regardless of breed, a puppy's disposition is perhaps his most important quality. It is, after all, what makes a puppy lovable and "livable." If the puppy's parents or grandparents are known to be snappy or aggressive, the puppy is likely to inherit those tendencies. That can lead to serious problems, such as the dog's becoming a biter, which can lead to eventual abandonment.

The three most common crate types: mesh on the left, wire on the right and fiberglass on top.

heavy plastic mesh; they are very lightweight and fold up into slim-line suitcases. However, a mesh crate might not be suitable for a pup with manic chewing habits or a large adult like the Curly.

Don't bother with a puppy-sized crate. Although your Curly-Coated Retriever will be a wee fellow when you bring him home, he will grow up in the blink of an eye and your puppy crate will be useless. Purchase a crate that will accommodate an adult Curly-Coated Retriever. A large crate of about 48 inches long by 30 inches wide by 36 inches high will fit him nicely; for the pup this can be partitioned with removable divider panels so he does not feel lost in a too-big crate.

BEDDING AND CRATE PADS
Your puppy will enjoy some type of soft bedding in his "room" (the crate), something he can snuggle

into to feel cozy and secure. Old towels or blankets are good choices for a young pup, since he may (and probably will) have a toileting accident or two in the crate or decide to chew on the bedding material. Once he is fully trained and out of the early chewing stage, you can replace the puppy bedding with a perma-nent crate pad if you prefer. Crate pads and other dog beds run the gamut from inexpensive to high-end doggie-designer styles, but don't splurge on the good stuff until you are sure that your puppy is reliable and won't tear it up or make a mess on it.

PUPPY TOYS
Just as infants and older children require objects to stimulate their minds and bodies, puppies need toys to entertain their curious brains, wiggly paws and achy teeth. A fun array of safe doggie toys will help satisfy your puppy's chewing instincts and distract him from gnawing on the

COST OF OWNERSHIP
The purchase price of your puppy is merely the first expense in the typical dog budget. Quality dog food, veterinary care (sickness and health maintenance), dog supplies and grooming costs will add up to big bucks every year. Can you adequately afford to support a canine addition to the family?

leg of your antique chair or your new leather sofa. Most puppy toys are cute and look as if they would be a lot of fun, but not all are necessarily safe or good for your puppy, so use caution when you go puppy-toy shopping.

Like all retriever breeds, Curlies are orally fixated and love to chew. Only the sturdiest toys should be offered to Curlies, puppies or adults. The best "chew-cifiers" are sturdy nylon and hard rubber bones, which are safe to gnaw on and come in sizes appropriate for all age groups and breeds. Be especially careful of natural bones, which can splinter or develop dangerous sharp edges; pups can easily swallow or choke on those bone splinters. Veterinarians often tell of surgical nightmares involving bits of splintered bone, because in addition to

the danger of choking, the sharp pieces can damage the intestinal tract.

Similarly, rawhide chews, while a favorite of most dogs and puppies, can be equally dangerous. Pieces of rawhide are easily swallowed after they get soft and gummy from chewing, and dogs have been known to choke on pieces of ingested rawhide. Rawhide chews should be offered only when you can supervise.

Soft woolly toys are special puppy favorites. They come in a wide variety of cute shapes and sizes; some look like little stuffed animals. Puppies love to shake them up and toss them about, or simply carry them around. Be careful of fuzzy toys that have button eyes or noses that your pup could chew off and swallow, and make sure that he does not disembowel a squeaky toy to remove the squeaker! Braided

This puppy will soon outgrow his crate. An adult-sized crate is a wiser investment as you will be able to use it at all stages of your Curly's life.

WHAT SIZE IS THE RIGHT SIZE?

When purchasing a crate, buy one that will fit an adult-size dog. Puppy crates are poor investments, since puppies quickly outgrow them. The crate should accommodate an adult dog in a standing position so that he has room to stand up, turn around and lie down comfortably. An even larger crate is fine but not necessary for the dog's comfort, as most of his crate time will be spent lying down and napping.

TOYS 'R SAFE

The vast array of tantalizing puppy toys is staggering. Stroll through any pet shop or pet-supply outlet and you will see that the choices can be overwhelming. However, not all dog toys are safe or sensible. Most very young puppies enjoy soft woolly toys that they can snuggle with and carry around. (It's time to replace these toys when the pup shreds them up!) Avoid toys that have buttons, tabs or other enhancements that can be chewed off and swallowed. Soft toys that squeak are fun, but make sure your puppy does not disembowel the toy and remove (and swallow) the squeaker. Toys that rattle or make noise can excite a puppy, but they present the same danger as the squeaky kind and so require supervision. Hard rubber toys that bounce can also entertain a pup, but make sure that the toy is too big for your pup to swallow.

rope toys are similar in that they are fun to chew and toss around, but they shred easily and the strings are easy to swallow. The strings are not digestible and, if the puppy doesn't pass them in his stool, he could end up at the vet's office. As with rawhides, your puppy should be closely monitored with rope toys.

If you believe that your pup has ingested a piece of one of his toys, check his stools for the next couple of days to see if he passes the item when he defecates. At the same time, also watch for signs of intestinal distress. A call to your veterinarian might be in order to get his advice and be on the safe side.

An all-time favorite toy for puppies (young and old!) is the empty gallon milk jug. Hard plastic juice containers—46 ounces or more—are also excellent. Such containers make lots of noise when they are batted about, and puppies go crazy with delight as they play with them. However, they don't often last very long, so be sure to remove and replace them when they get chewed up.

A word of caution about homemade toys: be careful with your choices of non-traditional play objects. Never use old shoes or socks, since a puppy cannot distinguish between the old ones on which he's allowed to chew and the new ones in your closet that are strictly off limits. That principle applies to anything that resembles something that you don't want your puppy to chew.

COLLARS

A lightweight nylon collar is the best choice for a very young pup. Quick-clip collars are easy to put on and remove, and they can be adjusted as the puppy grows. Introduce him to his collar as soon as he comes home to get him accustomed to wearing it. He'll get used to it quickly and won't mind a bit. Make sure that it is snug enough that it won't slip off, yet loose enough to be comfortable for the pup. You should be able to slip two fingers between the collar and his neck. Check the collar often, as puppies grow in spurts, and his collar can become too tight almost overnight. Choke collars are made for training but are not recommended for the

Curly-Coated Retriever. Such a training method should not be necessary with the breed, and they do not respond well to harsh physical correction.

Favorite toys for a Curly are those that can be used for retrieving games with his favorite playmate—you.

LEASHES

A 6-foot nylon lead is an excellent choice for a young puppy. It is lightweight and not as tempting to chew as a leather lead. You can switch to a 6-foot leather lead after your pup has grown and is used to walking politely on a lead. For initial puppy walks and house-training purposes, you should invest in a shorter lead so that you have more control over the puppy. At first, you don't want him wandering too far away from you, and when taking him out for toileting you will want to keep him in the specific area chosen for his potty spot.

Once the puppy is heel-trained with a traditional leash, you can consider purchasing a retractable lead. A retractable lead is excellent for walking adult dogs that are

CREATE A SCHEDULE

Puppies thrive on sameness and routine. Offer meals at the same time each day, take him out at regular times for potty trips and do the same for play periods and outdoor activity. Make note of when your puppy naps and when he is most lively and energetic, and try to plan his day around those times. Once he is house-trained and more predictable in his habits, he will be better able to tolerate changes in his schedule.

already leash-wise. This type of lead allows the dog to roam farther away from you and explore a wider area when out walking, and also retracts when you need to keep him close to you. Be sure to purchase one appropriate for your Curly's adult weight.

HOME SAFETY FOR YOUR PUPPY

The importance of puppy-proofing cannot be overstated. In addition to making your house comfortable for your Curly-Coated Retriever's arrival, you also must make sure

TOXIC PLANTS

Plants are natural puppy magnets, but many can be harmful, even fatal, if ingested by a puppy or adult dog. Scout your yard and home interior and remove any plants, bushes or flowers that could be even mildly dangerous. It could save your puppy's life. You can obtain a complete list of toxic plants from your veterinarian, at the public library or by looking online.

that your house is safe for your puppy before you bring him home. There are countless hazards in the owner's personal living environment that a pup can sniff, chew, swallow or destroy. Many are obvious; others are not. Do a thorough advance house check to remove or rearrange those things that could hurt your puppy, keeping any potentially dangerous items out of areas to which he will have access.

Electrical cords are especially dangerous, since puppies view them as irresistible chew toys. Unplug and remove all exposed cords or fasten them beneath baseboards where the puppy cannot reach them. Veterinarians and firefighters can tell you horror stories about electrical burns and house fires that resulted from puppy-chewed electrical cords. Consider this a most serious precaution for your puppy and the rest of your family.

Scout your home for tiny objects that might be seen at a pup's eye level. Keep medication bottles and cleaning supplies well out of reach, and do the same with waste baskets and other trash containers. It goes without saying that you should not use rodent poison or other toxic chemicals in any puppy area and that you must keep such containers safely locked up. You will be amazed at how many places a curious puppy can discover!

A Dog-Safe Home

The dog-safety police are taking you on a house tour. Let's go room by room and see how safe your own home is for your new pup. The following items are doggy dangers, so either they must be removed or the dog should be monitored or not have access to these areas.

Living Room

- house plants (some varieties are poisonous)
- fireplace or wood-burning stove
- paint on the walls (lead-based paint is toxic)
- lead drapery weights (toxic lead)
- lamps and electrical cords
- carpet cleaners or deodorizers

Outdoor

- swimming pool
- pesticides
- toxic plants
- lawn fertilizers

Bathroom

- blue water in the toilet bowl
- medicine cabinet (filled with potentially deadly bottles)
- soap bars, bleach, drain cleaners, etc.
- tampons

Kitchen

- household cleaners in the kitchen cabinets
- glass jars and canisters
- sharp objects (like kitchen knives, scissors and forks)
- garbage can (with remnants of good-smelling things like onions, potato skins, apple or pear cores, peach pits, coffee beans, etc.)
- leftovers or foods out on countertops (some "people foods" are toxic to dogs)

Garage

- antifreeze
- fertilizers (including rose foods)
- pesticides and rodenticides
- pool supplies (chlorine and other chemicals)
- oil and gasoline in containers
- sharp objects, electrical cords and power tools

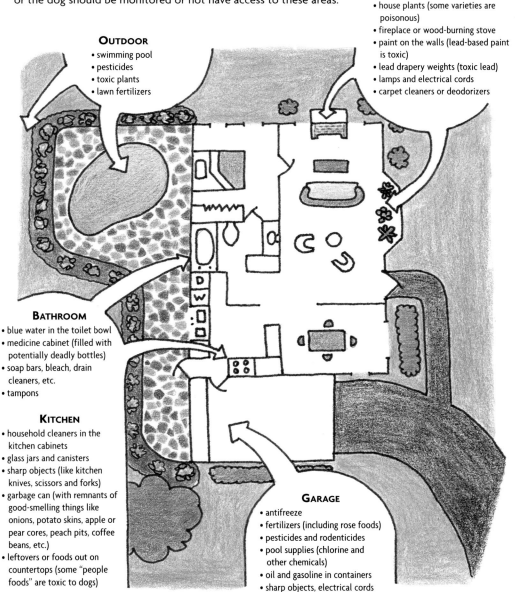

Once your house has cleared inspection, check your yard. A sturdy fence, well embedded into the ground, will give your dog a safe place to play and potty. Curly-Coated Retrievers are known for their expertise at the art of escape. You would be surprised at how crafty (and persistent) a Curly can be in figuring out how to dig and squeeze his way through holes or to jump or climb over a fence. A

PUPPY SHOTS

Puppies are born with natural antibodies that protect them from most canine diseases. They receive more antibodies from the colostrum in their mother's milk. These immunities wear off, however, and must be replaced through a series of vaccines. Puppy shots are given at 3- to 4-week intervals starting at 6 to 8 weeks of age through 12 to 16 weeks of age. Booster shots are given after one year of age, and every one to three years thereafter.

fence of at least 6 feet high above ground and anchored about a foot deep into the ground is the minimum for safe containment of your industrious and curious Curly. Check the fence periodically for necessary repairs. If there is a weak link or space to squeeze through, you can be sure a determined Curly-Coated Retriever will discover it.

The garage and shed can be hazardous places for a pup, as things like fertilizers, chemicals and tools are usually kept there. It's best to keep these areas off limits to the pup. Antifreeze is especially dangerous to dogs, as they find the taste appealing and it takes only a few licks from the driveway to kill a dog, puppy or adult, small breed or large.

VISITING THE VETERINARIAN
A good veterinarian is your Curly-Coated Retriever puppy's best health-insurance policy. If you do not already have a vet, ask friends and experienced dog people in your area for recommendations so that you can select a vet who is knowledgeable about retriever breeds before you bring your Curly-Coated Retriever puppy home. Also arrange for your puppy's first veterinary examination beforehand, since many vets do not have appointments immediately available, and your puppy should visit the vet within a day or so of coming home.

It's important to make sure that your puppy's first visit to the vet is a pleasant and positive one. The vet should take great care to befriend the pup and handle him gently to make their first meeting a positive experience. The vet will give the pup a thorough physical examination and set up a schedule for vaccinations and other necessary wellness visits. Be sure to show your vet any health and inoculation records, which you should have received from your breeder. Your vet is a great source of canine health information, so be sure to ask questions and take notes. Creating a health journal for your puppy will make a handy reference for his wellness and any future health problems that may arise.

MEETING THE FAMILY

Your Curly-Coated Retriever's homecoming is an exciting time for all members of the family, and it's only natural that everyone will be eager to meet him, pet him and play with him. However, for the puppy's sake, it's best to make these initial family meetings as uneventful as possible so that the pup is not overwhelmed with too much too soon. Remember, he has just left his dam and his littermates and is away from the breeder's home for the first time. Despite his fuzzy wagging tail, he is still apprehensive and

PUPPY PARASITES
Parasites are nasty little critters that live in or on your dog or puppy. Most puppies are born with ascarid roundworms, which are acquired from dormant ascarids residing in the dam. Other parasites can be acquired through contact with infected fecal matter. Take a stool sample to your vet for testing. He will prescribe a safe wormer to treat any parasites found in your puppy's stool. Always have a fecal test performed at your puppy's annual veterinary exam.

wondering where he is and who all these strange humans are. It's best to let him explore on his own and meet the family members as he feels comfortable. Let him investigate all the new smells, sights and sounds at his own pace. Children should be especially careful to not get overly excited, use loud voices or hug the pup too tightly. Be calm, gentle and affectionate, and be ready to comfort him if he appears frightened or uneasy.

Be sure to show your puppy his new crate during this first day home. Toss a treat or two inside the crate; if he associates the crate with food, he will associate the crate with good things. If he is comfortable with the crate, you can offer him his first meal inside it. Leave the door ajar so he can wander in and out as he chooses.

TEETHING TIME

All puppies chew. It's normal canine behavior. Chewing just plain feels good to a puppy, especially during the three- to five-month teething period when the adult teeth are breaking through the gums. Rather than attempting to eliminate such a strong natural chewing instinct, you will be more successful if you redirect it and teach your puppy what he may or may not chew. Correct inappropriate chewing with a sharp "No!" and offer him a chew toy, praising him when he takes it. Don't become discouraged. Chewing usually decreases after the adult teeth have come in.

FIRST NIGHT IN HIS NEW HOME

So much has happened in your Curly-Coated Retriever puppy's first day away from the breeder. He's had his first car ride to his new home. He's met his new human family and perhaps the other family pets. He has explored his new house and yard, at least those places where he is to be allowed during his first weeks at home. He may have visited his new veterinarian. He has eaten his first meal or two away from his dam and littermates. Surely that's enough to tire out an eight-week-old Curly-Coated Retriever pup—or so you hope!

It's bedtime. During the day, the pup investigated his crate, which is his new den and sleeping space, so it is not entirely strange to him. Line the crate with a soft towel or blanket that he can snuggle into and gently place him into the crate for the night. Some breeders send home a piece of bedding from where the pup slept with his littermates, and those familiar scents are a great comfort for the puppy on his first night without his siblings.

He will probably whine or cry. The puppy is objecting to the confinement and the fact that he is alone for the first time. This can be a stressful time for you as well as for the pup. It's important that you remain strong and don't let the puppy out of his crate to comfort him. He will fall asleep eventually. If you release him, the puppy will learn that crying means "out" and will continue that habit. You are laying the groundwork for future habits. Some breeders find that soft music can soothe a crying pup and help him get to sleep.

SOCIALIZING YOUR PUPPY

The first 20 weeks of your Curly-Coated Retriever puppy's life are the most important of his entire lifetime. A properly socialized puppy will grow up to be a confident and stable adult who will be a pleasure to live with and a welcome addition to the neighborhood.

The importance of socialization cannot be overemphasized. Research on canine behavior has proven that puppies who are not exposed to new sights, sounds, people and animals during their first 20 weeks of life will grow up to be timid and fearful, even aggressive, and unable to flourish outside of their familiar home environment.

THE CRITICAL SOCIALIZATION PERIOD

Canine research has shown that a puppy's 8th through 20th week is the most critical learning period of his life. This is when the puppy "learns to learn," a time when he needs positive experiences to build confidence and stability. Puppies who are not exposed to different people and situations outside the home during this period can grow up to be fearful and sometimes aggressive. This is also the best time for puppy lessons, since he has not yet acquired any bad habits that could undermine his ability to learn.

Socializing your puppy is not difficult and, in fact, will be a fun time for you both. Lead training goes hand in hand with socialization, so your puppy will be learning how to walk on a lead at the same time that he's meeting the neighborhood. Because the Curly-Coated Retriever is such a unique and fascinating breed, everyone will enjoy meeting "the new kid on the block." Give your Curly time to warm up to the new faces he meets. Take him for short walks, to the park and to other dog-friendly places where he will encounter new people, especially children. Puppies automatically recognize children as "little people" and are drawn to play with them. Just make sure that you supervise these meetings and that the children do not get too rough or encourage him to play too hard. An overzealous pup can often nip too hard, frightening the child and in turn making the puppy overly excited. A bad experience in puppyhood can impact a dog for life, so a pup that has a negative experience with a child may grow up to be shy or even aggressive around children.

Take your puppy along on your daily errands. Puppies are natural "people magnets," and most people who see your pup will want to pet him. All of these encounters will help to mold him into a confident adult dog. Likewise, you will soon feel like a

HAPPY CURLIES COME RUNNING

Never call your puppy or adult dog to come to you and then scold him or discipline him when he gets there. He will make a natural association between coming to you and being scolded, and he will think he was a bad dog for coming to you. He will then be reluctant to come whenever he is called. Always praise your Curly every time he comes to you.

second rounds of vaccinations before you expose him to other dogs or bring him to places that other dogs may frequent. Avoid dog parks and other strange-dog areas until your vet assures you that your puppy is fully immunized and resistant to the diseases that can be passed between canines. Discuss socialization with your breeder, as some breeders recommend socializing the puppy even before he has received all of his inoculations, depending on how outgoing the puppy may be.

LEADER OF THE PUPPY'S PACK

Like other canines, your puppy needs an authority figure, someone he can look up to and regard as the leader of his "pack." His first pack leader was his dam, who taught him to be polite and not chew too hard on her ears or nip at her muzzle. He learned those same lessons from his littermates. If he played too rough, they cried in pain and stopped the game, which sent an important message to the rowdy puppy.

confident, responsible dog owner, rightly proud of your mannerly Curly-Coated Retriever.

Be especially careful of your puppy's encounters and experiences during the eight- to ten-week-old period, which is also called the "fear period." This is a serious imprinting period, and all contact during this time should be gentle and positive. A frightening or negative event could leave a permanent impression that could affect his future behavior if a similar situation arises.

Also make sure that your puppy has received his first and

As puppies play together, they are also struggling to determine who will be the boss. Being pack animals, dogs need someone to be in charge. If a litter of puppies remained together beyond puppyhood, one of the pups would emerge as the strongest one, the one who calls the shots.

Once your puppy leaves the pack, he will look intuitively for a new leader. If he does not recognize you as that leader, he will try to assume that position for himself. Of course, it is hard to imagine your adorable Curly-Coated Retriever puppy trying to be in charge when he is so small and seemingly helpless. You must remember that these are natural canine instincts. Do not cave in and allow your pup to get the upper "paw"!

Just as socialization is so important during these first 20 weeks, so too is your puppy's early education. He was born without any bad habits. He does not know what is good or bad behavior. If he does things like nipping and digging, it's because he is having fun and doesn't know that humans consider these things as "bad." It's your job to teach him proper puppy manners, and this is the best time to accomplish that—before he has developed bad habits, since it is much more difficult to "unlearn" or correct unacceptable learned behavior than to teach good behavior from the start.

Make sure that all members of the family understand the importance of being consistent when training their new puppy. If you tell the puppy to stay off the sofa and your daughter allows him to cuddle on the couch to watch her favorite television show, your pup will be confused about what he is and is not allowed to do. Have a family conference before your pup comes home so that everyone understands the basic principles of puppy training and the rules you have set forth for the pup, and agrees to follow them.

The old saying that "an ounce of prevention is worth a pound of cure" is especially true when it comes to puppies. It is much easier to prevent inappropriate behavior than it is to change it. It's also easier and less stressful for the pup, since it will keep discipline to a minimum and create a more positive learning environment for him. That, in turn, will also be easier on you!

KEEP OUT OF REACH

Most dogs don't browse around your medicine cabinet, but accidents do happen! The drug acetaminophen, the active ingredient in certain popular over-the-counter pain relievers, can be deadly to dogs and cats if ingested in large quantities. Acetaminophen toxicity, caused by the dog's swallowing 15 to 20 tablets, can be manifested in abdominal pains within a day or two of ingestion, as well as liver damage. If you suspect your dog has swiped a bottle of medication, get the dog to the vet immediately so that the vet can induce vomiting and cleanse the dog's stomach.

The breeder's rapport with her puppies will tell you a lot about how the litter has been cared for. Dedication to and love of the breed are evident in how the puppies respond to the breeder's attention.

Here are a few commonsense tips to keep your belongings safe and your puppy out of trouble:

- Keep your closet doors closed and your shoes, socks and other apparel off the floor so your puppy can't get at them.
- Keep a secure lid on the trash container or put the trash where your puppy can't dig into it. He can't damage what he can't reach!
- Supervise your puppy at all times to make sure he is not getting into mischief. If he starts to chew the corner of the rug, you can distract him instantly by tossing a toy for him to fetch. You also will be able to whisk him outside when you notice that he is about to piddle on the carpet. If you can't see your puppy, you can't teach him or correct his behavior.

SOLVING PUPPY PROBLEMS

CHEWING AND NIPPING

Nipping at fingers and toes is normal puppy behavior. Chewing is also the way that puppies investigate their surroundings. Retrievers are oral breeds, and it's natural for them to want to put their mouths on things. However, you will have to teach your puppy that mouthing and chewing anything other than his toys is not acceptable. That won't happen overnight and at times puppy teeth will test your patience. However, if you allow nipping and chewing to continue, just think about the damage that a mature Curly can do with a full set of adult teeth.

Whenever your puppy nips your hand or fingers, cry out "Ouch!" in a loud voice, which should startle your puppy and stop him from nipping, even if only for a moment. Immediately distract him by offering a small treat or an appropriate toy for him to chew instead (which means having chew toys and puppy treats handy or in your pockets at all times). Praise him when he takes the toy and tell him what a good fellow he is. Praise is just as or even more important in puppy training as discipline and correction.

Puppies also tend to nip at children more often than adults, since they perceive little ones to be more vulnerable and more similar to their littermates. Teach your children appropriate responses to nipping behavior. If they are unable to handle it themselves, you may have to intervene. Puppy nips can be quite painful and a child's frightened reaction will only encourage a puppy to nip harder, which is a natural canine response. As with all other puppy situations, interaction between your Curly-Coated Retriever puppy and children should be supervised.

Chewing on objects, not just family members' fingers and ankles, is also normal canine behavior that can be especially tedious (for the owner, not the pup) during the teething period when the puppy's adult teeth are coming in. At this stage, chewing just plain feels good. Furniture legs and cabinet corners are common puppy favorites. Shoes and other personal items also taste pretty good to a pup.

The best solution is, once again, prevention. If you value

something, keep it tucked away and out of reach. You can't hide your dining-room table in a closet, but you can try to deflect the chewing by applying a bitter product made just to deter dogs from chewing. This spray-on substance is vile-tasting, although safe for dogs, and most puppies will avoid the forbidden object after one tiny taste. You also can apply the product to your leather leash if the puppy tries to chew on his lead during leash-training sessions.

Keep a ready supply of safe chews handy to offer your Curly-Coated Retriever as a distraction when he starts to chew on something that's a "no-no." Remember, at this tender age, he does not yet know what is permitted or forbidden, so you have to be "on call" every minute he's awake and on the prowl.

You may lose a treasure or two during puppy's growing-up period, and the furniture could sustain a nasty nick or two. These

Chewing is every puppy's favorite game. Discourage your pup from using his teeth in play or you will have an unruly adult to contend with.

ESTABLISH A ROUTINE
Routine is very important to a puppy's learning environment. To facilitate house-training, use the same exit/entrance door for potty trips and always take the puppy to the same place in the yard. The same principle of consistency applies to all other aspects of puppy training.

Curly puppies get sufficient exercise on their own, just being their curious selves. Keep a watchful eye on your little explorer.

can be trying times, so be prepared for those inevitable accidents and comfort yourself in knowing that this too shall pass.

JUMPING UP

Curly-Coated Retrievers retain puppy exuberance for their first few years of life, and puppies jump up—on you, your guests, your counters and your furniture. Just another normal part of growing up, and one you need to meet head-on before it becomes an ingrained habit. A two-year-old Curly "puppy" can easily knock someone down if he jumps up, and this kind of greeting can be quite intimidating and not likely appreciated by visitors to your home.

The key to jump correction is consistency. You cannot correct your Curly for jumping up on you today, then allow it to happen tomorrow by greeting him with hugs and kisses. As you have learned by now, consistency is critical to all puppy lessons.

For starters, try turning your back as soon as the puppy jumps.

Jumping up is a means of gaining your attention and, if the pup can't see your face, he may get discouraged and learn that he loses eye contact with his beloved master when he jumps up.

Leash corrections also work, and most puppies respond well to a leash tug if they jump. Grasp the leash close to the puppy's collar and give a quick tug downward, using the command "Off." Do not use the word "Down," since "Down" is used to teach the puppy to lie down, which is a separate action that he will learn during his education in the basic commands. As soon as the puppy has backed off, tell him to sit and immediately praise him for doing so. This will take many repetitions and won't be accomplished

BE CONSISTENT

Consistency is a key element, in fact is absolutely necessary, to a puppy's learning environment. A behavior (such as chewing, jumping up or climbing onto the furniture) cannot be forbidden one day and then allowed the next. That will only confuse the pup, and he will not understand what he is supposed to do. Just one or two episodes of allowing an undesirable behavior to "slide" will imprint that behavior on a puppy's brain and make that behavior more difficult to erase or change.

quickly, so don't get discouraged or give up; you must be even more persistent than your puppy.

A second method used for jump correction is the spritzer bottle. Fill a spray bottle with water mixed with a bit of lemon juice or vinegar. As soon as puppy jumps, command him "Off" and spritz him with the water mixture. Of course, that means having the spray bottle handy whenever or wherever jumping usually happens.

Yet a third method to discourage jumping is grasping the puppy's paws and holding them gently but firmly until he struggles to get away. Wait a brief moment or two, then release his paws and give him a command to sit. He should eventually learn that jumping gets him into an uncomfortable predicament.

Children are major victims of puppy jumping, since puppies view little people as ready targets for jumping up as well as nipping. If your children (or their friends) are unable to dispense jump corrections, you will have to intervene and handle it for them.

Important to prevention is also knowing what you should *not* do. Never kick your Curly (for any reason, not just for jumping) or knock him in the chest with your knee. That maneuver could actually harm your puppy. Vets can tell you stories about puppies

who suffered broken bones after being banged about when they jumped up.

PUPPY WHINING
Puppies often cry and whine, just as infants and little children do. It's their way of telling us that they are lonely or in need of attention. Your puppy will miss his littermates and will feel insecure when

A SMILE'S WORTH A MILE
Don't embark on your puppy's training course when you're not in the mood. Never train your puppy if you're feeling grouchy or impatient with him. Subjecting your puppy to your bad mood is a bad move. Your pup will sense your negative attitude, and neither of you will enjoy the session or have any measure of success. Always begin and end your training sessions on a happy note.

DIGGING OUT

Some Curlies love to dig and they are certainly good at it. Digging is considered "self-rewarding behavior" because it's fun! Of all the digging solutions offered by the experts, most are only marginally successful and none are guaranteed to work. The best cure is prevention, which means removing the dog from the offending site when he digs as well as distracting him when you catch him digging so that he turns his attentions elsewhere. That means that you have to supervise your dog's yard time. An unsupervised digger can create havoc with your landscaping or, worse, run away!

he is left alone. You may be out of the house or just in another room, but he will still feel alone. During these times, the puppy's crate should be his personal comfort station, a place all his own where he can feel safe and secure. Once he learns that being alone is okay and not something to be feared, he will settle down without crying or objecting. You might want to leave a radio on while he is crated, as the sound of human voices can be soothing and will give the impression that people are around.

Give your puppy a favorite sturdy chew toy to entertain him whenever he is crated. You will both be happier: the puppy because he is safe in his den and you because he is quiet, safe and

not getting into puppy escapades that can wreak havoc in your house or cause him danger.

To make sure that your puppy will always view his crate as a safe and cozy place, never, *ever* use the crate as punishment. That's the best way to turn the crate into a negative place that the pup will want to avoid. Sure, you can use the crate for your own peace of mind if your puppy is getting into trouble and needs some "time out." Just don't let him know that! Never scold the pup and immediately place him into the crate. Count to ten, give him a couple of hugs and maybe a treat, then scoot him into his crate.

It's also important not to make a big fuss when he is released from the crate. That will make getting out of the crate more appealing than being in the crate, which is just the opposite of what you are trying to achieve.

"COUNTER SURFING"

What we like to call "counter surfing" is a normal extension of jumping and usually starts to happen as soon as a puppy realizes that he is big enough to stand on his hind legs and investigate the good stuff on the kitchen counter or the coffee table. Once again, you have to be there to prevent it! As soon as you see your Curly-Coated Retriever even start to raise himself up, startle him with a sharp "No!" or "Aaahh, aaahh!" If he succeeds and manages to get one or both paws on the forbidden surface, smack those paws (firmly but gently) and tell him "Off!" Guide him back to the floor and as soon as he's back on all four paws, command him to sit and praise at once.

For surf prevention, make sure to keep any tempting treats or edibles out of reach, where your Curly-Coated Retriever can't see or smell them. It's the old rule of prevention yet again.

FOOD GUARDING

Occasionally, the true "chow hound" will become protective of his food, which is one dangerous step toward other aggressive behavior. Food guarding is obvious: your puppy will growl, snarl or even attempt to bite you if you approach his food bowl or put your hand into his pan while he's eating.

This behavior is not acceptable, and very preventable! If your puppy is an especially voracious eater, sit next to him occasionally while he eats and dangle your fingers in his food bowl to encourage him to eat more slowly (this is for health reasons, too). Don't feed him in a corner, where he could feel possessive of his eating space. Rather, place his food bowl in an open area of your kitchen where you are in close proximity. Occasionally remove his food in mid-meal, tell him he's a good boy and return his bowl.

MEET AND MINGLE
Puppies need to meet people and see the world if they are to grow up confident and unafraid. Take your puppy with you on everyday outings and errands. On-lead walks around the neighborhood and to the park offer the pup good exposure to the goings-on of his new human world. Avoid areas frequented by other dogs until your puppy has had his full round of puppy shots; ask your vet when your pup will be properly protected. Arrange for your puppy to meet new people of all ages every week.

If your pup becomes possessive of his food, look for other signs of future aggression, like guarding his favorite toys or refusing to obey obedience commands that he knows. Consult an obedience trainer for help in reinforcing obedience so your Curly-Coated Retriever will fully understand that *you* are the boss.

By keeping to a consistent schedule, your puppy will be in sync with the family's routine in no time! This little guy already knows when it's time to go out and waits by the door to remind his owner.

CURLY-COATED RETRIEVER

Adding a Curly-Coated Retriever to your household means adding a new family member who will need your care each and every day. When your Curly pup first comes home, you will start a routine with him so that, as he grows up, your dog will have a daily schedule just as you do. The aspects of your dog's daily care will likewise become regular parts of your day, so you'll both have a new schedule. Dogs learn by consistency and thrive on routine: regular times for meals, exercise, grooming and potty trips are just as important for your dog as they are for you! Your dog's schedule will depend much on your family's daily routine, but remember that you now have a new member of the family who is part of your day every day!

FEEDING

Feeding your dog the best diet is based on various factors, including age, activity level, overall condition and size of breed. When you visit the breeder, he will share with you his advice about the proper diet for your dog based on his experience with the breed and the foods with which he has had success. Likewise, your vet will be a helpful source of advice throughout the dog's life and will aid you in planning a diet for optimal health.

FEEDING THE PUPPY

Of course, your pup's very first food will be his dam's milk. There may be special situations in which pups fail to nurse, necessitating that the breeder hand-feed them with a formula, but for the most part pups spend the first weeks of life nursing from their dam. The breeder weans the pups by gradually introducing solid foods and decreasing the milk meals. Pups may even start themselves off on the weaning process, albeit inadvertently, if they snatch bites from their mom's food bowl.

By the time the pups are ready for new homes, they are fully weaned and eating a good puppy food. As a new owner, you may be thinking, "Great! The breeder has taken care of the hard part." Not so fast.

A Curly puppy's first year of life is the time when much of his growth and development takes place, although the breed keeps growing at a slower pace for several more years. This first year

SWITCHING FOODS

There are certain times in a dog's life when it becomes necessary to switch his food; for example, from puppy to adult food and then from adult to senior-dog food. Additionally, you may decide to feed your pup a different type of food from what he received from the breeder, and there may be "emergency" situations in which you can't find your dog's normal brand and have to offer something else temporarily. Anytime a change is made, for whatever reason, the switch must be done gradually. You don't want to upset the dog's stomach or end up with a picky eater who refuses to eat something new. A tried-and-true approach is, over the course of about a week, to mix a little of the new food in with the old, increasing the proportion of new to old as the days progress. At the end of the week, you'll be feeding his regular portions of the new food, and he will barely notice the change.

is a delicate time, and diet plays a huge role in proper skeletal and muscular formation. Improper diet and exercise habits can lead to damaging problems that will compromise the dog's health and movement for his entire life. That being said, new owners should not worry needlessly. With the myriad types of food formulated specifically for growing pups of different-sized breeds, dog-food manufacturers have taken much of the guesswork out of feeding your puppy well. Since growth-food formulas are designed to provide the nutrition that a growing puppy needs, it is unnecessary and, in fact, can prove harmful to add supplements to the diet. Research has shown that too much of certain vitamin supplements and minerals predispose a dog to skeletal problems. It's by no means a case of "if a little is good, a lot is better." At every stage of your dog's life, too much or too little in the way of nutrients can be harmful, which is why a manufactured complete food is the easiest way to know that your dog is getting what he needs.

Because of a young pup's small body and accordingly small digestive system, his daily portion will be divided up into small meals throughout the day. This can mean starting off with three or more meals a day and decreasing the number of meals as the pup matures, progressing to a lifelong schedule of two meals a day on a morning/evening schedule. This is much healthier than one large daily portion; smaller meals help reduce the risk of the potentially deadly condition known as bloat (gastric torsion).

Regarding the feeding schedule, feeding the pup at the same times and in the same place each day is important for housebreaking purposes and establishing the dog's everyday routine. As for the amount to feed, growing puppies generally need proportionately more food per body weight than their adult counterparts, but a pup should never be allowed to gain excess weight. Dogs of all ages should be kept in proper body condition, but extra weight can strain a pup's developing frame, causing skeletal problems.

Watch your pup's weight as he grows and, if the recommended amounts seem to be too much or too little for your pup, consult the vet about appropriate dietary changes. Keep in mind that treats, although small, can quickly add up throughout the day, contributing unnecessary calories. Treats are fine when used prudently; opt for dog treats specially formulated to be healthy or for nutritious snacks like small pieces of cheese or cooked chicken.

FEEDING THE ADULT DOG

For the adult (meaning physically mature) dog, feeding properly is about maintenance, not growth. While the slow-maturing Curly keeps growing until three or four years of age, he can be switched to an adult-maintenance food at around one year old. Again, correct weight is a concern. Your dog should appear fit and should have an evident "waist." His ribs should not be protruding (a sign of being underweight), but they should be covered by only a slight layer of fat. Under normal circumstances, an adult dog can be maintained fairly easily with a high-quality nutritionally complete adult-formula food.

Factor treats into your dog's overall daily caloric intake, and

NOT HUNGRY?

No dog in his right mind would turn down his dinner, would he? If you notice that your dog has lost interest in his food, there could be any number of causes. Dental problems are a common cause of appetite loss, one that is often overlooked. If your dog has a toothache, a loose tooth or sore gums from infection, chances are it doesn't feel so good to chew. Think about when you've had a toothache! If your dog does not approach the food bowl with his usual enthusiasm, look inside his mouth for signs of a problem. Whatever the cause, you'll want to consult your vet so that your chow hound can get back to his happy, hungry self as soon as possible.

This Curly puppy certainly approaches his bowl eagerly!

addition to a consistent routine, regular mealtimes allow the owner to practice the daily bloat preventives regarding feeding and exercise as well as to see how much his dog is eating. If the dog seems never to be satisfied or, likewise, becomes uninterested in his food, the owner will know right away that something is wrong and can consult the vet.

avoid offering table scraps. Not only are certain "people foods," like chocolate, nuts, raisins, grapes, onions and significant quantities of garlic, toxic to dogs but feeding from your plate also encourages begging and overeating. Overweight dogs are more prone to health problems. Research has even shown that obesity takes years off a dog's life. With that in mind, resist the urge to overfeed and over-treat. Don't make unnecessary additions to your dog's diet, whether with tidbits or with extra vitamins and minerals.

The amount of food needed for proper maintenance will vary depending on the individual dog's activity level, but you will be able to tell whether the daily portions are keeping him in good shape. With the wide variety of good complete foods available, choosing what to feed is largely a matter of personal preference. Just as with the puppy, the adult dog should have consistency in his mealtimes and feeding place. In

DIET DON'TS
- Got milk? Don't give it to your dog! Dogs cannot tolerate large quantities of cows' milk, as they do not have the enzymes to digest lactose.
- You may have heard of dog owners who add raw eggs to their dogs' food for a shiny coat or to make the food more palatable, but consumption of raw eggs too often can cause a deficiency of the vitamin biotin.
- Avoid feeding table scraps, as they will upset the balance of the dog's complete food. Additionally, fatty or highly seasoned foods can cause upset canine stomachs.
- Do not offer raw meat to your dog. Raw meat can contain parasites; it also is high in fat.
- Vitamin A toxicity in dogs can be caused by too much raw liver, especially if the dog already gets enough vitamin A in his balanced diet, which should be the case.
- Bones like chicken, pork chop and other soft bones are not suitable, as they easily splinter.

What Is "Bloat" and How Do I Prevent it?

You likely have heard the term "bloat," which refers to gastric torsion (gastric dilatation/volvulus), a potentially fatal condition. As it is directly related to feeding and exercise practices, a brief explanation here is warranted. The term *dilatation* means that the dog's stomach is filled with air, while *volvulus* means that the stomach is twisted around on itself, blocking the entrance/exit points. Dilatation/volvulus is truly a deadly combination, although they also can occur independently of each other. An affected dog cannot digest food or pass gas, and blood cannot flow to the stomach, causing accumulation of toxins and gas along with great pain and rapidly occurring shock.

Many theories exist on what exactly causes bloat, but we do know that deep-chested breeds are more prone and that the risk doubles after seven years of age. Activities like eating a large meal, gulping water, strenuous exercise too close to mealtimes or a combination of these factors can contribute to bloat, though not every case is directly related to these more well-known causes. With that in mind, we can focus on incorporating simple daily preventives and knowing how to recognize the symptoms. In addition to the tips presented in this book, ask your vet about how to prevent and recognize bloat. An affected dog needs immediate veterinary attention, as death can result quickly. Signs include obvious restlessness/discomfort, crying in pain, drooling/excessive salivation, unproductive attempts to vomit or relieve himself, hardened abdomen, visibly bloated appearance and collapsing. Do not wait: get to the vet or emergency veterinary clinic *right away* if you see any of these symptoms. The vet will confirm by x-ray if the stomach is bloated with air; if so, the dog must be treated surgically *immediately*.

As varied as the causes of bloat are the tips for prevention, but some common preventive methods follow:
• Feed two or three small meals daily rather than one large one;
• Do not feed water before, after or with meals, but allow access to water at all other times;
• Never permit rapid eating or gulping of water;
• No exercise for the dog at least two hours before and (especially) after meals;
• Feed high-quality food with adequate protein, adequate fiber content and not too much fat and carbohydrate;
• Explore herbal additives, enzymes or gas-reduction products (only under a vet's advice) to encourage a "friendly" environment in the dog's digestive system;
• Avoid foods and ingredients known to produce gas;
• Avoid stressful situations for the dog, especially at mealtimes;
• Make dietary changes gradually, over a period of a few weeks;
• Do not feed dry food only; and avoid any kibble that expands greatly when wet;
• Although the role of genetics as a causative of bloat is not known, many breeders do not breed from previously affected dogs;
• Sometimes owners are advised to have gastroplexy (stomach stapling) performed on their dogs as a preventive measure.
Pay attention to your dog's behavior and any changes that could be symptomatic of bloat. Your dog's life depends on it!

DIETS FOR THE AGING DOG

A good rule of thumb is that once a dog has reached 75% of his expected lifespan, he has reached "senior citizen" or geriatric status. Your Curly-Coated Retriever will be considered a senior at about 7–8 years of age; based on his size and breed-specific factors, he has a projected lifespan of about 10–12 years.

What does aging have to do with your dog's diet? No, he won't get a discount at the local diner's early-bird special. Yes, he will require some dietary changes to accommodate the changes that come along with increased age. One change is that the older dog's dietary needs become more similar to that of a puppy. Specifically, dogs can metabolize more protein as youngsters and seniors than in the adult-maintenance stage. Discuss with your vet whether you need to switch to a higher-protein or senior-formulated food or whether your current adult-dog food contains sufficient nutrition for the senior.

Watching the dog's weight remains essential, even more so in the senior stage. Older dogs are already more vulnerable to illness, and obesity only contributes to their susceptibility to problems. As the older dog becomes less active and, thus, exercises less, his regular portions may cause him to gain weight. At this point, you may consider decreasing his daily food intake or switching to a reduced-calorie food. As with other changes, you should consult your vet for advice. Dietary changes depend on the individual dog's metabolism, activity level and lifestyle.

DON'T FORGET THE WATER!

Regardless of what type of food your Curly eats, there's no doubt that he needs plenty of water. Fresh cold water, in a clean bowl, should be freely available to your dog. There are special circumstances, such as during puppy housebreaking, when you will want to monitor your pup's water intake so that you will be able to predict when he will need to relieve himself, but water must be available to him nonetheless. Water is essential for hydration and proper body function just as it is in humans.

You will get to know how much your dog typically drinks in

HOLD THE ONIONS

Sliced, chopped or grated; dehydrated, boiled, fried or raw; pearl, Spanish, white or red: onions can be deadly to your dog. The toxic effects of onions in dogs are cumulative for up to 30 days. A serious form of anemia, called Heinz body anemia, affects the red blood cells of dogs that have eaten onions. For safety (and better breath), dogs should avoid chives and scallions as well.

a day. Of course, in the heat or if exercising vigorously, he will be more thirsty. However, if he begins to drink noticeably more water for no apparent reason, this could signal any of various problems, and you are advised to consult your vet.

A word of warning concerning your deep-chested Curly's water intake: he should never be allowed to gulp water or consume large quantities of water, especially around mealtimes and exercise times. Do not offer water with or around mealtimes, but allow free access to water at all other times. This will encourage him to quench his thirst as needed and prevent him from drinking too much at one time. These simple daily precautions can go a long way in protecting your dog from the potentially fatal bloat.

EXERCISE

All dogs require some form of exercise, regardless of breed. A sedentary lifestyle is as harmful to a dog as it is to a person. The Curly is definitely an active breed that enjoys exercise, but you don't have to be an Olympic athlete to provide your dog with a sufficient amount of activity! Exercising your Curly can be enjoyable and healthy for both of you; remember to allow adequate quiet time for your Curly before and after mealtimes and periods of activity.

Brisk walks will stimulate heart rates and build muscle for both dog and owner. As the dog reaches adulthood, the speed and distance of the walks can be

QUENCHING HIS THIRST

Is your dog drinking more than normal and trying to lap up everything in sight? Excessive drinking has many different causes. Obvious causes for a dog's being thirstier than usual are hot weather and vigorous exercise. However, if your dog is drinking more for no apparent reason, you could have cause for concern. Serious conditions like kidney or liver disease, diabetes and various types of hormonal problems can all be indicated by excessive drinking. If you notice your dog's being excessively thirsty, contact your vet at once. Hopefully there will be a simpler explanation, but the earlier a serious problem is detected, the sooner it can be treated, with a better rate of cure.

For the puppy, on-lead walks should be kept short but are important for showing the pup how to walk (and how *not* to walk!) on a leash.

your Curly to run, but not run away!

Swimming is also an excellent form of exercise for a water breed like the Curly-Coated Retriever. Curlies naturally take to water and are very talented swimmers. You will need to ensure that the swimming area is safe, but once you've found an appropriate place, your Curly will not need convincing to jump right in! Of course, puppies should be introduced to water slowly, but it will not take them long to become confident in the water.

Bear in mind that an overweight dog should never be suddenly over-exercised; instead he should be encouraged to increase exercise slowly. Also remember that not only is exercise

increased as long as they are both kept reasonable and comfortable for both of you. Keep in mind that a Curly puppy should not engage in jumping or high-impact exercise before one year of age to prevent causing stress to his developing joints.

Play sessions and free-running time in the fenced yard under your supervision also are sufficient forms of exercise for the Curly-Coated Retriever. Fetching games can be played indoors or out; these are excellent for giving your dog active play that he will enjoy while engaging in something that comes naturally to him—retrieving! When your Curly runs after the ball or object, praise him for picking it up and encourage him to bring it back to you for another throw. Never go to the object and pick it up yourself, or you'll soon find that you are the one retrieving the objects rather than the dog! Remember, for off-leash activity, you must be in a securely enclosed area. You want

TWO'S COMPANY

One surefire method of increasing your adult dog's exercise plan is to adopt a second dog. If your dog is well socialized, he should take to his new canine pal in no time and soon the two will be giving each other lots of activity and exercise as they play, romp and explore together. Most owners agree that two dogs are hardly much more work than one. If you cannot afford a second dog, get together with a friend or neighbor who has a well-trained dog. Your Curly should enjoy the company of a new four-legged playmate!

essential to keep the dog's body fit, it is essential to his mental well-being. A bored Curly will find something to do, which often manifests itself in some type of destructive behavior. In this sense, exercise is essential for the owner's mental well-being as well!

GROOMING

ROUTINE CARE
The Curly could easily be called a wash-and-wear dog because of his easy-care, tightly curled coat. Daily care is unnecessary; the coat should never be brushed or combed out, since that would stretch and frizz the coat. Brushing or combing with a wide-toothed comb is necessary only twice a year during the shedding periods in spring and fall. Only a slight bit of year-round shedding occurs as the hair shafts stop growing, die and eventually fall out.

Most owners keep their Curlies groomed with bathing about three or four times a year, which helps to control normal coat loss and keeps the dog clean and tidy. The curly coat is frequently oily, which tends to attract and accumulate dead hair and dirt. Bathing removes the dust and allergens from the coat, which is important for Curly owners who are allergic to such things.

Frequent swimming sessions will also aid in removing dust accumulation from the coat.

SCOOTING HIS BOTTOM
Here's a doggy problem that many owners tend to neglect. If your dog is scooting his rear end around the carpet, he probably is experiencing anal-sac impaction or blockage. The anal sacs are the two grape-sized glands on either side of the dog's vent that should empty on their own during bowel movements. If impacted, the dog cannot empty these glands, which become filled with a foul-smelling material. The dog may attempt to lick the area to relieve the pressure. He may also rub his anus on your walls, furniture or floors.

Don't neglect your dog's rear end during grooming sessions. By squeezing both sides of the anus with a soft cloth, you can express some of the material in the sacs. If the material is pasty and thick, you likely will need the assistance of a veterinarian. Vets know how to express the glands and can show you how to do it correctly without hurting the dog or spraying yourself with the unpleasant liquid.

Hunters rarely bathe their Curlies during hunting season so that the coats will retain their natural oil and thus provide more protection from the elements. All hunting dogs should be checked after each outdoor session for burrs and other debris that may have lodged in the coat during field work.

A light coat conditioner can be sprayed on to freshen up the coat between baths.

During shedding a comb can be used, but only one with widely spaced teeth. Never "comb out" the coat.

Instead of brushing and combing, a Curly's coat is tidied up by trimming away any scraggly hairs.

Although the breed standard does not require extensive grooming for the show ring, most judges expect the dogs to be tidied up before entering the show ring. Exhibitors usually scissor excess hair from the tail, ears and legs. Pet owners often maintain their dogs' coats in this manner too.

BATHING

As mentioned, Curlies need to be bathed only a few times a year, possibly more often if your dog gets into something messy or if he starts to smell like a dog. Field dogs are bathed even less frequently. Bathing too often can have negative effects on the skin and coat, removing natural oils and causing dryness.

If you give your dog his first bath when he is young, he will become accustomed to the process. With the Curly, anything involving water is first nature, and Curly puppies take little coaxing to enjoy time in the bath—limiting the fun is the usual challenge.

Before bathing the dog, have the items you'll need close at hand. First, decide where you will bathe the dog. You should have a tub or basin with a non-slip surface. Puppies can even be bathed in a sink. In warm weather, some like to use a portable pool in the yard, although you'll want to make sure your dog doesn't head for the nearest dirt pile following his bath! You will also need a hose or shower spray to wet the coat thoroughly, a shampoo formulated for dogs and a few absorbent towels. Human shampoos are too harsh for dogs' coats and will dry them out.

Before wetting the dog, remove any debris from his coat. Make sure he is at ease in the tub and have the water at a comfortable temperature. Begin bathing by wetting the coat all the way down to the skin. Massage in the shampoo, keeping it away from his face

Curlies are easy to bathe! A bath outdoors in warm weather will seem more like playtime than grooming time to this water-loving retriever.

and eyes. Rinse him thoroughly, again avoiding the eyes and ears, as you don't want to get water into the ear canals. A thorough rinsing is important, as shampoo residue is drying and itchy to the dog. After rinsing, wrap him in a towel to absorb most of the moisture. The coat can then finish drying naturally. You should keep the dog indoors and away from drafts until he is completely dry.

NAIL CLIPPING

Having their nails trimmed is not on many dogs' lists of favorite things to do. With this in mind, you will need to accustom your puppy to the procedure at a young age so that he will sit still (well, as still as he can) for his pedicures. Long nails can cause the dog's feet to spread, which is not good for

---

WATER SHORTAGE

No matter how well behaved your dog is, bathing is always a project! Nothing can substitute for a good warm bath, but owners do have the option of giving their dogs "dry" baths. Pet shops sell excellent products, in both powder and spray forms, designed for spot-cleaning your dog. These dry shampoos are convenient for touch-up jobs when you don't have the time to bathe your dog in the traditional way.

Muddy feet, messy behinds and smelly coats can be spot-cleaned and deodorized with a "wet-nap"-style cleaner. On those days when your dog insists on rolling in fresh goose droppings and there's no time for a bath, a spot bath can save the day. These pre-moistened wipes are also handy for other grooming needs like wiping faces, ears and eyes and freshening tails and behinds.

Since the coat is water-resistant, it will take some extra effort to thoroughly wet the coat before applying shampoo and then to give a complete rinsing.

him; likewise, long nails can hurt if they unintentionally scratch, not good for you!

Some dogs' nails are worn down naturally by regular walking on hard surfaces, so the frequency with which you clip depends on your individual dog. Look at his nails from time to time and clip as needed; a good way to know when it's time for a trim is if you hear your dog clicking as he walks across the floor.

There are several types of nail clippers and even electric nail-grinding tools made for dogs; first we'll discuss using the clipper. To start, have your clipper ready and some doggie treats on hand. You want your pup to view his nail-clipping sessions in a positive light, and what better way to

convince him than with food? You may want to enlist the help of an assistant to comfort the pup and offer treats as you concentrate on the clipping itself. The guillotine-type clipper is thought of by many

THE MONTHLY GRIND

If your dog doesn't like the feeling of nail clippers or if you're not comfortable using them, you may wish to try an electric nail grinder. This tool has a small sandpaper disc on the end that rotates to grind the nails down. Some feel that using a grinder reduces the risk of cutting into the quick; this can be true if the tool is used properly. Usually you will be able to tell where the quick is before you get to it. A benefit of the grinder is that it creates a smooth finish on the nails so that there are no ragged edges.

Because the tool makes noise, your dog should be introduced to it before the actual grinding takes place. Turn it on and let your dog hear the noise; turn it off and let him inspect it with you holding it. Use the grinder gently, holding it firmly and progressing a little at a time until you reach the proper length. Look at the nail as you grind so that you do not go too short. Stop at any indication that you are nearing the quick. It will take a few sessions for both you and the puppy to get used to the grinder, but you should soon find it easy and convenient to use.

as the easiest type to use; the nail tip is inserted into the opening, and blades on the top and bottom snip it off in one clip.

Start by grasping the pup's paw; a little pressure on the foot pad causes the nail to extend, making it easier to clip. Clip off a little at a time. If you can see the "quick," which is a blood vessel that runs through each nail, you will know how much to trim, as you do not want to cut into the quick. On that note, if you do cut the quick, which will cause bleeding, you can stem the flow of blood with a styptic pencil or other clotting agent. If you mistakenly nip the quick, do not panic or fuss, as this will cause the pup to be afraid. Simply reassure the pup, stop the bleeding and move on to the next nail. Don't be discouraged; you will become a professional canine pedicurist with practice.

You may or may not be able to see the quick, so it's best to just

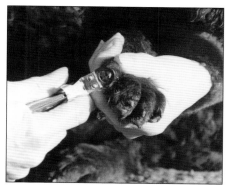

Most dogs do not enjoy having the nails clipped. A guillotine-type clipper made for dogs is the easiest type of clipper to use.

clip off a small bit at a time. If you see a dark dot in the center of the nail, this is the quick and your cue to stop clipping. Tell the puppy he's a "good boy" and offer a piece of treat with each nail. You can also use nail-clipping time to examine the footpads, making sure that they are not dry and cracked and that nothing has become embedded in them.

The nail grinder, the other choice, is many owners' first choice. Accustoming the puppy to the sound of the grinder and sensation of the buzz presents fewer challenges than the clipper, and there's no chance of cutting through the quick. Use the grinder on a low setting and always talk soothingly to your dog. He won't mind his salon visit, and he'll have nicely polished nails as well.

Insert only the nail tip into the clipper and take it off in one quick clip.

EAR CLEANING
While keeping your dog's ears clean unfortunately will not cause him to "hear" your commands any

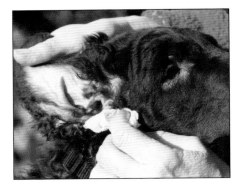

Clean the ears with an ear-cleansing formula and a soft wipe or cotton ball.

better, it will protect him from ear infection and ear-mite infestation. In addition, a dog's ears are vulnerable to waxy build-up and to collecting foreign matter from the outdoors. Look in your dog's ears regularly to ensure that they look pink, clean and otherwise healthy. Even if they look fine, an odor in the ears signals a problem and means it's time to call the vet.

A Curly who swims frequently should have his ears checked and cleaned every day to prevent fungus growth and other ear prob-

lems from occurring. Regular use of an ear cleaner will also keep excess ear wax from accumulating. For those that don't swim often, cleaning once a week should be sufficient. Using a cotton ball or pad, and never probing into the ear canal, wipe the ear gently. You can use an ear-cleansing liquid or powder available from your vet or pet-supply store; alternatively, you might prefer to use home-made solutions with ingredients like one part white vinegar and one part hydrogen peroxide. Ask your vet about home remedies before you attempt to concoct something on your own!

Keep your dog's ears free of excess hair by plucking it as needed. If done gently, this will be painless for the dog. Look for wax, brown droppings (a sign of ear mites), redness or any other abnormalities. At the first sign of a problem, contact your vet so that he can prescribe an appropriate medication.

EYE CARE
During grooming sessions, pay extra attention to the condition of your dog's eyes. If the area around the eyes is soiled or if tear staining has occurred, there are various cleaning agents made especially for this purpose. Look at the dog's eyes to make sure no debris has entered; dogs with large eyes and those who spend a lot of time outdoors are especially prone to this.

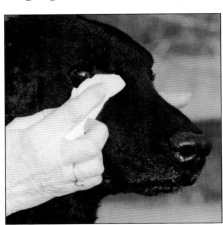

The areas around the eyes can be gently cleaned with a damp cloth. There also are cleaning formulas made for this purpose.

The signs of an eye infection are obvious: mucus, redness, puffiness, scabs or other signs of irritation. If your dog's eyes become infected, the vet will likely prescribe an antibiotic ointment for treatment. If you notice signs of more serious problems, such as opacities in the eye, which usually indicate cataracts, consult the vet at once. Taking time to pay attention to your dog's eyes will alert you in the early stages of any problem so that you can get your dog treatment as soon as possible. You could save your dog's sight!

IDENTIFICATION AND TRAVEL

ID FOR YOUR DOG

You love your Curly-Coated Retriever and want to keep him safe. Of course you take every precaution to prevent his escaping from the yard or becoming lost or

stolen. You have a sturdy high fence and you always keep your dog on lead when out and about in public places. If your dog is not properly identified, however, you are overlooking a major aspect of his safety. We hope to never be in a situation where our dog is missing, but we should practice prevention in the unfortunate case that this happens; identification greatly increases the chances of your dog's being returned to you.

There are several ways to identify your dog. First, the traditional dog tag should be a staple in your dog's wardrobe, attached to his everyday collar. Tags can be made of sturdy plastic and various metals and should include your contact information so that a person who finds the dog can get in touch with you right away to arrange his return. Many people today enjoy the wide range of decorative tags available, so have fun and create a tag to match your

Your Curly-Coated Retriever should *never* be loose in the car when you are driving with him. This is important for the dog's safety as well as that of the driver and passengers.

> **PET OR STRAY?**
> Besides the obvious benefit of providing your contact information to whoever finds your lost dog, an ID tag makes your dog more approachable and more likely to be recovered. A strange dog wandering the neighborhood without a collar and tags will look like a stray, while the collar and tags indicate that the dog is someone's pet. Even if the ID tags become detached from the collar, the collar alone will make a person more likely to pick up the dog.

dog's personality. Of course, it is important that the tag stays on the collar, so have a secure "O"-ring attachment. Many hunters often use the type of tag that slides right onto the collar or nylon collars that have the contact information woven into it in a different color.

In addition to the ID tag, which every dog should wear even if identified by another method, two other forms of identification have become popular: microchipping and tattooing. In microchipping, a tiny scannable chip is painlessly inserted under the dog's skin. The number is registered to you so that, if your lost dog turns up at a clinic or shelter, the chip can be scanned to retrieve your contact information.

The advantage of the microchip is that it is a permanent form of ID, but there are some factors to consider. Several different companies make microchips, and not all are compatible with the others' scanning devices. It's best to find a company with a universal microchip that can be read by scanners made by other companies as well. It won't do any good to have the dog chipped if the information cannot be retrieved. Also, not every humane society, shelter and clinic is equipped with a scanner, although more and more facilities are equipping themselves. In fact, many shelters microchip dogs that they adopt out to new homes.

In the US, there are five or six major microchip manufacturers as well as a few databases. The American Kennel Club's Companion Animal Recovery unit works in conjunction with HomeAgain™ Companion Animal Retrieval System (Schering-Plough).

Because the microchip is not visible to the eye, the dog must wear a tag that states that he is microchipped so that whoever picks him up will know to have him scanned. The tag usually also contains the registry's phone number and the dog's microchip ID number. He of course also should have a tag with your contact information in case his chip's information cannot be retrieved. Humane societies and veterinary clinics offer microchipping service, which is usually very affordable.

Though less popular than microchipping, tattooing is another permanent method of ID for dogs. Most vets perform this service, and there are also clinics that perform dog tattooing. This is also an affordable procedure and one that will not cause much discomfort for the dog. It is best to put the tattoo in a visible area, such as the ear, to deter theft. It is sad to say that there are cases of dogs' being stolen and sold to research laboratories, but such laboratories will not accept tattooed dogs.

To ensure that the tattoo is effective in aiding your dog's return to you, the tattoo number must be registered with a national organization. That way, when someone finds a tattooed dog, a phone call to the registry will quickly match the dog with his owner.

HIT THE ROAD

Car travel with your Curly-Coated Retriever may be limited to necessity only, such as trips to the vet, or you may bring your dog along almost everywhere you go. This will depend much on your individual dog and how he reacts to rides in the car. You can begin desensitizing your dog to car travel as a pup so that it's something that he's used to. Still, some dogs suffer from motion sickness. Your vet may prescribe a medication for this if trips in the car pose a problem for your dog. At the very least, you will need to get him to the vet, so he will need to tolerate these trips with the least amount of hassle possible.

Start taking your pup on short trips, maybe just around the block to start. If he is fine with short trips, lengthen your rides a little at a time. Start to take him on your errands or just for drives around town. By this time it will be easy to tell whether your dog is a born traveler or would prefer staying at home when you are on the road.

Of course, safety is a concern for dogs in the car. First, he must travel securely, not left loose to roam about the car where he could be injured or distract the driver. A young pup can be held by a passenger initially but should soon graduate to a travel crate, which can be the same crate he uses in the home if it fits in your car. Other options include a car harness (like a seat belt for dogs) and partitioning the back of the car with a gate made for this purpose.

Bring along what you will need for the dog. He should wear his collar and ID tags, of course, and you should bring his leash, water (and food if a long trip) and clean-up materials for potty breaks and in case of motion sickness. Always keep your dog on his leash when you make stops, and never leave him alone in the car. Many a dog has died from the heat inside a closed car; this does not take much time at all, even in mild weather. A dog left alone inside a car can also be a target for thieves.

Visit local boarding facilities and choose one with which you are comfortable long before you need its services. A knowledgeable and attentive staff, clean accommodations and good reputation are among the priorities to consider.

Once he's well-versed in the basics, the Curly can be trained for work in the field, where he will feel right at home.

TRAINING YOUR
CURLY-COATED RETRIEVER

BASIC TRAINING PRINCIPLES: PUPPY VS. ADULT

There's a big difference between training an adult dog and training a young puppy. With a young puppy, everything is new! At eight to ten weeks of age, he will be experiencing many things, and he has nothing with which to compare these experiences. Up to this point, he has been with his dam and littermates, not one-on-one with people except in his interactions with his breeder and visitors to the litter.

When you first bring the puppy home, he is eager to please you. This means that he accepts doing things your way. During the next couple of months, he will absorb the basis of every-thing he needs to know for the rest of his life. This early age is even referred to as the "sponge" stage. After that, as the puppy grows up, it's up to you to rein-force good manners by building on the foundation that you've established. Once your puppy is reliable in basic commands and behavior and has reached the appropriate age, you may gradu-ally introduce him to some of the interesting sports, games and activities available to pet owners and their dogs.

Raising your puppy is a family affair. Each member of the family must know what rules to set forth for the puppy and how to use the same one-word commands to mean exactly the same thing every time. Even if yours is a large family, one person will soon be considered by the pup to be the leader, the alpha person in his pack, the "boss" who must be obeyed. Often that highly regarded person turns out to be the one who feeds the puppy. Food ranks very high on the puppy's list of important things! That's why your puppy is rewarded with small treats along with verbal praise

A natural retriever, the Curly responds instinctively to training for hunting tasks.

when he responds to you correctly. Curlies respond best to positive reinforcement in training.

TEACHER'S PET

Dogs are individuals, not robots, with many traits basic to their breed. Some, bred to work alone, are independent thinkers; others rely on you to call the shots. If you have enrolled in a training class, your instructor can offer alternative methods of training based on your individual dog's instincts and personality. You may benefit from using a different type of collar or switching to a class with different kinds of dogs.

As the puppy learns to do what you want him to do, the food rewards are gradually eliminated and only the praise remains. If you were to keep up with the food treats, you could have two problems on your hands—an obese dog and a beggar.

Training begins the minute your Curly-Coated Retriever puppy steps through the doorway of your home, so don't make the mistake of putting the puppy on the floor and telling him by your actions to "Go for it! Run wild!" Even if this is your first puppy, you must act as if you know what you're doing: be the boss. An uncertain pup may be terrified to move, while a bold one will be ready to take you at your word and start plotting to destroy the house! Before you collected your puppy, you decided where his own special place would be, and that's where to put him when you first arrive home. Give him a house tour after he has investigated his area and had a nap and a bathroom "pit stop."

It's worth mentioning here that, if you've adopted an adult dog that is completely trained to your liking, lucky you! You're off the hook! However, if that dog spent his life up to this point in a kennel, or even in a good home but without any real training, be prepared to tackle the job ahead. An adult dog with no previous training cannot be blamed for not knowing what he was never taught. While the dog is trying to understand and learn your rules, at the same time he has to unlearn many of his previously self-taught habits and general view of the world.

Working with a professional trainer will speed up your progress with an adopted adult dog. You'll need patience, too. Some new rules may be close to impossible for the dog to accept. After all, he's been successful so far by doing everything his way! (Patience again.) He may agree with your instruction for a few days and then slip back into his old ways, so you must be just as consistent and understanding in your teaching as you would be with a puppy. (More patience needed yet again!) Your dog has to learn to pay attention to

BASIC PRINCIPLES OF DOG TRAINING

1. Start training early. A young puppy is ready, willing and able.
2. Timing is your all-important tool. Praise at the exact time that the dog responds correctly. Pay close attention.
3. Patience is almost as important as timing!
4. Repeat! The same word has to mean the same thing every time.
5. In the beginning, praise all correct behavior verbally, along with treats and petting.

your voice, your family, the daily routine, new smells, new sounds and, in some cases, even a new climate.

One of the most important things to find out about a newly adopted adult dog is his reaction to children (yours and others), strangers and your friends, and how he acts upon meeting other dogs. If he was not socialized with dogs as a puppy, this could be a major problem. This does not mean that he's a "bad" dog, a vicious dog or an aggressive dog; rather, it means that he has no idea how to read another dog's body language. There's no way for

You can be sure that your Curly will pay attention when food is involved, but don't give in to a beggar!

Mischief and the Curly pup go hand-in-hand! Patience and a sense of humor are keys to training success.

him to tell whether the other dog is a friend or foe. Survival instinct takes over, telling him to attack first and ask questions later. A properly raised Curly should not be an aggressive dog, but lack of socialization can have negative effects on a dog of any breed. This definitely calls for professional help and, even then, may not be a behavior that can be corrected 100% reliably (or even at all). If you have a puppy, this is why it is so very important to introduce your young puppy properly to other puppies and "dog-friendly" adult dogs.

HOUSE-TRAINING YOUR CURLY-COATED RETRIEVER

Dogs are tactility-oriented when it comes to house-training. In other words, they respond to the surface on which they are given approval to eliminate. The choice is yours (the dog's version is in parenthe-

ses): The lawn (including the neighbors' lawns)? A bare patch of earth under a tree (where people like to sit and relax in the summertime)? The concrete steps or patio (all sidewalks, garages and basement floors)? The curbside (watch out for cars)? A small area of crushed stone in a corner of the yard (mine!)? The latter is the best choice if you can manage it, because it will remain strictly for the dog's use and is easy to keep clean.

You can start out with paper-training indoors and switch over to an outdoor surface as the puppy matures and gains control over his need to eliminate. For the nay-sayers, don't worry—this won't

WHO'S TRAINING WHOM?
Dog training is a black-and-white exercise. The correct response to a command must be absolute, and the trainer must insist on completely accurate responses from the dog. A trainer cannot command his dog to sit and then settle for the dog's melting into the down position. Often owners are so pleased that their dogs "did something" in response to a command that they just shrug and say, "OK, down" even though they wanted the dog to sit. You want your dog to respond to the command without hesitation: he must respond at that moment and correctly every time.

BE UPSTANDING!
You are the dog's leader. During training, stand up straight so your dog looks up at you, and therefore up *to* you. Say the command words distinctly, in a clear, declarative tone of voice. (No barking!) Give rewards only as the correct response takes place (remember your timing!). Praise, smiles and treats are "rewards" used to positively reinforce correct responses. Don't repeat a mistake. Just change to another exercise—you will soon find success!

part-time job. It requires someone to be home all day.

If that seems overwhelming or impossible, do a little planning. For example, plan to pick up your puppy at the start of a vacation period. If you can't get home in the middle of the day, plan to hire a dog-sitter or ask a neighbor to come over to take the pup outside, feed him his lunch and then take him out again about ten or so minutes after he's eaten. Also make arrangements with that or another person to be your "emergency"

The Curly retains the attitude of a puppy in the body of an adult for several years—this can be challenging yet endearing to those who appreciate the breed's unique qualities.

mean that the dog will soil on every piece of newspaper lying around the house. You are training him to go outside, remember? Starting out by paper-training often is the only choice for a city dog.

WHEN YOUR PUPPY'S "GOT TO GO"
Your puppy's need to relieve himself is seemingly non-stop, but signs of improvement will be seen each week. From 8 to 10 weeks old, the puppy will have to be taken outside every time he wakes up, about 10–15 minutes after every meal and after every period of play—all day long, from first thing in the morning until his bedtime. That's a total of ten or more trips per day to teach the puppy where it's okay to relieve himself. With that schedule in mind, you can see that house-training a young puppy is not a

Secure in his wire crate, this Curly pup is safe and out of trouble—yet still involved in the family fun.

to run about, but he is safe from dangerous things like electrical cords, heating units, trash baskets or open kitchen-supply cabinets. Place the pen where the puppy will not get a blast of heat or air conditioning.

In the pen, you can put a few toys, his bed (which can be his crate if the dimensions of pen and crate are compatible) and a few layers of newspaper in one small corner, just in case. A water bowl can be hung at a convenient height on the side of the ex-pen so it won't become a splashing pool for an innovative puppy. His food dish can go on the floor, next to the

contact if you have to stay late on the job. Remind yourself—repeatedly—that this hectic schedule improves as the puppy gets older.

HOME WITHIN A HOME
Your Curly-Coated Retriever puppy needs to be confined to one secure, puppy-proof area when no one is able to watch his every move. Generally, the kitchen is the place of choice because the floor is washable. Likewise, it's a busy family area that will accustom the pup to a variety of noises, everything from pots and pans to the telephone, blender and dishwasher. He will also be enchanted by the smell of your cooking (and will never be critical when you burn something). An exercise pen (also called an "expen," a puppy version of a playpen) within the room of choice can help confine a young pup. He can see out and has a certain amount of space in which

EXTRA! EXTRA!
The headlines read: "Puppy Piddles Here!" Breeders commonly use newspapers to line their whelping pens, so puppies learn to associate newspapers with relieving themselves. Do not use newspapers to line your pup's crate, as this will signal to your puppy that it is OK to urinate in his crate. If you choose to paper-train your puppy, you will layer newspapers on a section of the floor near the door he uses to go outside. You should encourage the puppy to use the papers to relieve himself, and bring him there whenever you see him getting ready to go. Little by little, you will reduce the size of the newspaper-covered area so that the puppy will learn to relieve himself "on the other side of the door."

CANINE DEVELOPMENT SCHEDULE

It is important to understand how and at what age a puppy develops into adulthood. If you are a puppy owner, consult this Canine Development Schedule to determine the stage of development your puppy is currently experiencing. This knowledge will help you as you work with the puppy in the weeks and months ahead.

PERIOD	AGE	CHARACTERISTICS
FIRST TO THIRD	BIRTH TO SEVEN WEEKS	Puppy needs food, sleep and warmth and responds to simple and gentle touching. Needs mother for security and disciplining. Needs littermates for learning and interacting with other dogs. Pup learns to function within a pack and learns pack order of dominance. Begin socializing pup with adults and children for short periods. Pup begins to become aware of his environment.
FOURTH	EIGHT TO TWELVE WEEKS	Brain is fully developed. Pup needs socializing with outside world. Remove from mother and littermates. Needs to change from canine pack to human pack. Human dominance necessary. Fear period occurs between 8 and 12 weeks. Avoid fright and pain.
FIFTH	THIRTEEN TO SIXTEEN WEEKS	Training and formal obedience should begin. Less association with other dogs, more with people, places, situations. Period will pass easily if you remember this is pup's change-to-adolescence time. Be firm and fair. Flight instinct prominent. Permissiveness and over-disciplining can do permanent damage. Praise for good behavior.
JUVENILE	FOUR TO EIGHT MONTHS	Another fear period about seven to eight months of age. It passes quickly, but be cautious of fright and pain. Sexual maturity reached. Dominant traits established. Dog should understand sit, down, come and stay by now.

NOTE: THESE ARE APPROXIMATE TIME FRAMES. ALLOW FOR INDIVIDUAL DIFFERENCES IN PUPPIES.

In your "happy" voice, use the word "Crate" every time you put the pup into his den. If he's new to a crate, toss in a small biscuit for him to chase the first few times. At night, after he's been outside, he should sleep in his crate. The crate may be kept in his designated area at night or, if you want to be sure to hear those wake-up yips in the morning, put

The Curly puppy will fit into your home environment quite naturally. Be certain you have a safe area prepared for him before he comes home.

water bowl. Someone will have to still keep an eye on the pup in his pen—remember the Curly's penchant for escaping. A crate is the answer for the puppy when no one is at home or if you are busy in another part of the house.

Crates are something that pet owners are at last getting used to for their dogs. Wild or domestic canines have always preferred to sleep in den-like safe spots, and that is exactly what the crate provides. How often have you seen adult dogs that choose to sleep under a table or chair even though they have full run of the house? It's the den connection.

SOMEBODY TO BLAME

House-training a puppy can be frustrating for the puppy and the owner alike. The puppy does not instinctively understand the difference between defecating on the pavement outside and on the ceramic tile in the kitchen. He is confused and frightened by his human's exuberant reactions to his natural urges. The owner, arguably the more intelligent of the duo, is also frustrated that he cannot convince his puppy to obey his commands and instructions.

In frustration, the owner may struggle with the temptation to discipline the puppy, scold him or even strike him on the rear end. Harsh corrections are unnecessary and inappropriate, serving to defeat your purpose in gaining your puppy's trust and respect. Don't blame your nine-week-old puppy. Blame yourself for not being 100% consistent in the puppy's lessons and routine. The lesson here is simple: try harder and your puppy will succeed.

the crate in a corner of your bedroom. However, don't make any response whatsoever to whining or crying. If he's completely ignored, he'll settle down and get to sleep.

Good bedding for a young puppy is an old folded bath towel or an old blanket, something that is easily washable and disposable if necessary ("accidents" will happen!). Never put newspaper in the puppy's crate. Also, those old ideas about adding a clock to replace his mother's heartbeat, or a hot-water bottle to replace her warmth, are just that—old ideas. The clock could drive the puppy nuts, and the hot-water bottle could end up as a very soggy waterbed! An extremely good breeder would have introduced your puppy to the crate by letting two pups sleep together for a couple of nights, followed by several nights alone. How thankful you will be if you found that breeder!

Safe toys in the pup's crate or area will keep him occupied, but monitor their condition closely. Discard any toys that show signs of being chewed to bits. Squeaky parts, bits of stuffing or plastic or any other small pieces can cause intestinal blockage or possibly choking if swallowed.

PROGRESSING WITH POTTY-TRAINING
After you've taken your puppy out and he has relieved himself in

TIDY BOY
Clean by nature, dogs do not like to soil their dens, which in effect are their crates or sleeping quarters. Unless not feeling well, dogs will not defecate or urinate in their crates. Crate training capitalizes on the dog's natural desire to keep his den clean. Be conscientious about giving the puppy as many opportunities to relieve himself outdoors as possible. Reward the puppy for correct behavior. Praise him and pat him whenever he "goes" in the correct location. Even the tidiest of puppies can have potty accidents, so be patient and dedicate more energy to helping your puppy achieve a clean lifestyle.

the area you've selected, he can have some free time with the family as long as there is someone responsible for watching him. That doesn't mean just someone in the same room who is watching TV or busy on the computer, but one person who is doing nothing other than keeping an eye on the pup, playing with him on the floor and helping him understand his position in the pack.

This first taste of freedom will let you begin to set the house rules. If you don't want the dog on the furniture, now is the time to prevent his first attempts to jump up onto the couch. The word to use in this case is "Off,"

not "Down." "Down" is the word you will use to teach the down position, which is something entirely different.

Most corrections at this stage come in the form of simply distracting the puppy. Instead of telling him "No" for "Don't chew the carpet," distract the chomping puppy with a toy and he'll forget about the carpet.

As you are playing with the pup, do not forget to watch him closely and pay attention to his body language. Whenever you see him begin to circle or sniff, take the puppy outside to relieve himself. If you are starting out by paper-training, put him back into his confined area on the newspapers. In either case, praise him as he eliminates while he actually is *in the act* of relieving himself. Three seconds after he has finished is too late! You'll be praising him for running toward you, picking up a toy or whatever he may be doing at that moment, and that's not what you want to be praising him for. Timing is a vital tool in all dog training. Use it.

Remove soiled newspapers immediately and replace them with clean ones. You may want to take a small piece of soiled paper and place it in the middle of the new clean papers, as the scent will attract him to that spot when it's time to go again. That scent attraction is why it's so important to clean up any messes made in the house by using a product specially made to eliminate the odor of dog urine and droppings. Regular household cleansers won't do the trick. Pet shops sell the best pet deodorizers. Invest in the largest container you can find.

Scent attraction eventually will lead your pup to his chosen spot outdoors; this is the basis of outdoor training. When you take your puppy outside to relieve himself, use a one-word command such as "Outside" or "Go-potty" (that's one word to the puppy!) as you pick him up and attach his leash. Then put him down in his area. If you cannot carry him, snap the leash on quickly and lead him to his spot. Now comes the hard part—hard for you, that is. Just stand there until he urinates and defecates. Move him a few feet in one direction or another if he's just sitting there, looking at you, but remember that this is neither playtime nor time for a walk. This is strictly a busi-

ness trip! Then, as he circles and squats (remember your timing!), give him a quiet "Good dog" as praise. If you start to jump for joy, ecstatic over his performance, he'll do one of two things: either he will stop mid-stream, as it were, or he'll do it again for you—in the house—and expect you to be just as delighted!

Give him five minutes or so and, if he doesn't go in that time, take him back indoors to his confined area and try again in another ten minutes, or immediately if you see him sniffing and circling. By careful observation, you'll soon work out a successful schedule.

Accidents, by the way, are just that—accidents. Clean them up quickly and thoroughly, without comment, after the puppy has been taken outside to finish his business and then put back into his area or crate. If you witness an accident in progress, say "No!" in a stern voice and get the pup outdoors immediately. No punishment is needed. You and your puppy are just learning each other's language, and sometimes it's easy to miss a puppy's message. Chalk it up to experience and watch more closely from now on.

KEEPING THE PACK ORDERLY
Discipline is a form of training that brings order to life. For example, military discipline is

POTTY COMMAND
Most dogs love to please their masters; there are no bounds to what dogs will do to make their owners happy. The potty command is a good example of this theory. If toileting on command makes the master happy, then more power to him. Puppies will obligingly piddle if it really makes their keepers smile. Some owners can be creative about which word they will use to command their dogs to relieve themselves. Some popular choices are "Potty," "Tinkle," "Piddle," "Let's go," "Hurry up" and "Toilet." Give the command every time your puppy goes into position and the puppy will begin to associate his business with the command.

what allows the soldiers in an army to work as one. Discipline is a form of teaching and, in dogs, is the basis of how the successful pack operates. Each member knows his place in the pack and all respect the leader, or alpha

SMILE WHEN YOU ORDER ME AROUND!

While trainers recommend practicing with your dog every day, it's perfectly acceptable to take a "mental health day" off. It's better not to train the dog on days when you're in a sour mood. Your bad attitude or lack of interest will be sensed by your dog, and he will respond accordingly. Studies show that dogs are well tuned-in to their humans' emotions. Be conscious of how you use your voice when talking to your dog. Raising your voice or shouting will only erode your dog's trust in you as his trainer and master.

dog. It is essential for your puppy that you establish this type of relationship, with you as the alpha, or leader. It is a form of social coexistence that all canines recognize and accept. Discipline, therefore, is never to be confused with punishment. When you teach your puppy how you want him to behave, and he behaves properly and you praise him for it, you are disciplining him with a form of positive reinforcement.

For a dog, rewards come in the form of praise, a smile, a cheerful tone of voice, a few friendly pats or a rub of the ears. Rewards are also small food treats. Obviously, that does not mean bits of regular dog food. Instead, treats are very small bits of special things like cheese or pieces of soft dog treats. The idea is to reward the dog with some-thing very small that he can taste and swallow, providing instant positive reinforcement. If he has to take time to chew the treat, he will have forgotten what he did to earn it by the time he is finished.

Your puppy should never be physically punished. The displeasure shown on your face and in your voice is sufficient to signal to the pup that he has done something wrong. He wants to please everyone higher up on the social ladder, especially his leader, so a scowl and harsh voice will take care of the error. Growling out the word "Shame!"

when the pup is caught in the act of doing something wrong is better than the repetitive "No." Some dogs hear "No" so often that they begin to think it's their name! By the way, do not use the dog's name when you're correcting him. His name is reserved to get his attention for something pleasant about to take place.

There are punishments that have nothing to do with you. For example, your dog may think that chasing cats is one reason for his existence. You can try to stop it as much as you like but without success, because it's such fun for the dog. But one good hissing, spitting, swipe of a cat's claws across the dog's nose will put an end to the game forever. Intervene only when your dog's eyeball is seriously at risk. Cat scratches can cause permanent damage to an innocent but annoying puppy.

SHOULD WE ENROLL?

If you have the means and the time, you should definitely take your dog to obedience classes. Begin with puppy kindergarten classes in which puppies of all sizes learn basic lessons while getting the opportunity to meet and greet each other; it's as much about socialization as it is about good manners. What you learn in class you can practice at home. And if you goof up in practice, you'll get help in the next session.

PUPPY KINDERGARTEN

COLLAR AND LEASH

Before you begin your Curly-Coated Retriever puppy's education, he must be used to his collar and leash. Choose a collar for your puppy that is secure, but not heavy or bulky. He won't enjoy training if he's uncomfortable. A flat buckle collar is fine for everyday wear and for initial puppy training. For older dogs, there are several types of training collars such as the martingale, which is a double loop that tightens slightly around the neck, or the head collar, which is similar to a horse's halter. Do not use a chain choke collar with your Curly as a puppy or adult.

A lightweight 6-foot woven cotton or nylon training leash is preferred by most trainers because

A small barrier won't keep this pup from paying his feline housemate a visit. Baby gates, pens and the like must be tall and sturdy enough to truly contain pup in his safe area.

Keeping your pup in a confined dog-proof area is about housebreaking and puppy safety as well as preventing puppy teeth from damaging your belongings.

it is easy to fold up in your hand and comfortable to hold because there is a certain amount of give to it. There are lessons where the dog will start off 6 feet away from you at the end of the leash. The leash used to take the puppy outside to relieve himself is shorter because you don't want him to roam away from his area. The shorter leash will also be the one to use when you walk the puppy.

If you've been wise enough to enroll in a puppy kindergarten training class, suggestions will be made as to the best collar and leash for your young puppy. I say "wise" because your puppy will be in a class with puppies in his age range (up to five months old) of all breeds and sizes. It's the perfect way for him to learn the right way (and the wrong way) to

interact with other dogs as well as their people. You cannot teach your puppy how to interpret another dog's sign language. For a first-time puppy owner, these socialization classes are invaluable. For experienced dog owners, they are a real boon to further training.

ATTENTION

You've been using the dog's name since the minute you collected him from the breeder, so you should be able to get his attention by saying his name—with a big smile and in an excited tone of voice. His response will be the puppy equivalent of "Here I am! What are we going to do?" Your immediate response (if you haven't guessed by now) is "Good dog." Rewarding him at the moment he pays attention to you teaches him the proper way to respond when he hears his name.

KEEP IT SIMPLE—AND FUN

Keep your lessons simple, interesting and user-friendly. Fun breaks help you both. Spend two minutes or ten teaching your puppy, but practice only as long as your dog enjoys what he's doing and is focused on pleasing you. If he's bored or distracted, stop the training session after any correct response (always end on a high note!). After a few minutes of playtime, you can go back to "hitting the books."

EXERCISES FOR A BASIC CANINE EDUCATION

THE SIT EXERCISE

There are several ways to teach the puppy to sit. The first one is to catch him whenever he is about to sit and, as his backside nears the floor, say "Sit, good dog!" That's positive reinforcement and, if your timing is sharp, he will learn that what he's doing at that second is connected to your saying "Sit" and that you think he's clever for doing it.

Another method is to start with the puppy on his leash in front of you. Show him a treat in the palm of your right hand. Bring your hand up under his nose and, almost in slow motion, move your hand up and back so his nose goes up in the air and his head tilts back as he follows the treat in your hand. At that point, he will have to either sit or fall over, so as his back legs buckle under, say "Sit, good dog," and then give him the treat and lots of praise. You may have to begin with your hand lightly running up his chest, actually lifting his chin up until he sits. Some (usually older) dogs require gentle pressure on their hindquarters with the left hand, in which case the dog should be on your left side. Puppies generally do not appreciate this physical dominance.

After a few times, you should be able to show the dog a treat in

the open palm of your hand, raise your hand waist-high as you say "Sit" and have him sit. Once again, you have taught him two things at the same time. Both the

The dog should respond naturally to the sit command. If he needs a little encouragement, you can guide him gently into the position.

first, when the doorbell rings or when you stop to speak to someone on the street.

THE DOWN EXERCISE

Before beginning to teach the down command, you must consider how the dog feels about this exercise. To him, "down" is a submissive position. Being flat on the floor with you standing over him is not his idea of fun. It's up to you to let him know that, while it may not be fun, the reward of your approval is worth his effort.

Start with the puppy on your left side in a sit position. Hold the leash right above his collar in your left hand. Have an extra-special treat, such as a small piece of cooked chicken or hot dog, in your right hand. Place it at the end of the pup's nose and steadily move your hand down and

verbal command and the motion of the hand are signals for the sit. Your puppy is watching you almost more than he is listening to you, so what you do is just as important as what you say.

Don't save any of these drills only for training sessions. Use them as much as possible at odd times during a normal day. The dog should always sit before being given his food dish. He should sit to let you go through a doorway

> **SIT AROUND THE HOUSE**
>
> "Sit" is the command you'll use most often. Your pup objects when placed in a sit with your hands, so try the "bringing the food up under his chin" method. Better still, catch him in the act! Your dog will sit on his own many times throughout the day, so let him know that he's doing the "Sit" by pairing the word with his action and rewarding him. Praise him and have him sit for everything—toys, connecting his leash, his dinner, before going out the door, etc.

DOWN

"Down" is a harsh-sounding word and a submissive posture in dog body language, thus presenting two obstacles in teaching the down command. When the dog is about to flop down on his own, tell him "Good down." Pups that are not good about being handled learn better by lowering food in front of them. A dog that trusts you can be gently guided into position. When you give the command "Down," be sure to say it sweetly!

forward along the ground. Hold the leash to prevent a sudden lunge for the food. As the puppy goes into the down position, say "Down" very gently.

The difficulty with this exercise is twofold: it's both the submissive aspect and the fact that most people say the word "Down" as if they were drill sergeants in charge of recruits! So issue the command sweetly, give him the treat and have the pup maintain the down position for several seconds. If he tries to get up immediately, place your hands on his shoulders and press down gently, giving him a very quiet "Good dog." As you progress with this lesson, increase the "down time" until he will hold it until you say "Okay" (his cue for release). Practice this one in the house at various times throughout the day.

By increasing the length of time during which the dog must maintain the down position, you'll find many uses for it. For example, he can lie at your feet in the vet's office or anywhere that both of you have to wait, when you are on the phone, while the family is eating and so forth. If you progress to training for competitive obedience, he'll already be all set for the exercise called the "long down."

THE STAY EXERCISE

You can teach your Curly-Coated Retriever to stay in the sit, down and stand positions. To teach the sit/stay, have the dog sit on your left side. Hold the leash at waist level in your left hand and let the dog know that you have a treat in your closed right hand. Step

Proceed to the down/stay only after the dog has learned the down command. Practice commands in an enclosed area that is free from distractions.

Off-leash training should only be done in safely enclosed areas and only after the particular command has been learned reliably on leash.

when you return and he holds the sit/stay. Increase the distance that you walk away from him before turning until you reach the length of your training leash. But don't rush it! Go back to the beginning if he moves before he should. No matter what the lesson, never be upset by having to back up for a few days. The repetition and practice are what will make your dog reliable in these commands. It won't do any good to move on to something more difficult if the command is not mastered at the

forward on your right foot as you say "Stay." Immediately turn and stand directly in front of the dog, keeping your right hand up high so he'll keep his eye on the treat hand and maintain the sit position for a count of five. Return to your original position and offer the reward.

Increase the length of the sit/stay each time until the dog can hold it for at least 30 seconds without moving. After about a week of success, move out on your right foot and take two steps before turning to face the dog. Give the "Stay" hand signal (left palm back toward the dog's head) as you leave. He gets the treat

TIPS FOR TRAINING AND SAFETY

1. Whether on- or off-leash, practice only in a fenced area.
2. Remove the training collar when the training session is over.
3. Don't try to break up a dogfight.
4. "Come," "Leave it" and "Wait" are safety commands.
5. The dog belongs in a crate or behind a barrier when riding in the car.
6. Don't ignore the dog's first sign of aggression. Aggression only gets worse, so take it seriously.
7. Keep the faces of children and dogs separated.
8. Pay attention to what the dog is chewing.
9. Keep the vet's number near your phone.
10. "Okay" is a useful release command.

easier levels. Above all, even if you do get frustrated, never let your puppy know! Always keep a positive, upbeat attitude during training, which will transmit to your dog for positive results.

The down/stay is taught in the same way once the dog is completely reliable and steady with the down command. Again, don't rush it. With the dog in the down position on your left side, step out on your right foot as you say "Stay." Return by walking around in back of the dog and into your original position. While you are training, it's okay to murmur something like "Hold on" to encourage him to stay put. When the dog will stay without moving when you are at a distance of 3 or 4 feet, begin to increase the length of time before you return. Be sure he holds the down on your return until you say "Okay." At that point, he gets his treat—just so he'll remember for next time that it's not over until it's over.

THE COME EXERCISE

No command is more important to the safety of your Curly-Coated Retriever than "Come." It is what you should say every single time you see the puppy running toward you: "Albie, come! Good dog." During playtime, run a few feet away from the puppy and turn and tell him to "Come" as he is already running to you. You can

FEAR AGGRESSION
Of the several types of aggression, the one brought on by fear is the most difficult for people to comprehend and to deal with. Aggression to protect food, or any object the dog perceives as his, is more easily understood. Fear aggression is quite different. The dog shows fear, generally for no apparent reason. He backs off, cowers or hides under the bed. If he's on lead, he will hide behind your leg and lash out unexpectedly. No matter how you approach him, he will bite. A fear-biter attacks with great speed and instantly retreats. Don't shout at him or go near him. Don't coddle, sympathize or try to protect him. To him, that's a reward. As with other forms of aggression, get professional help.

go so far as to teach your puppy two things at once if you squat down and hold out your arms. As the pup gets close to you and you're saying "Good dog," bring your right arm in about waist high. Now he's also learning the hand signal, an excellent device should you be on the phone when you need to get him to come to you! You'll also both be one step ahead when you enter obedience classes.

When the puppy responds to your well-timed "Come," try it with the puppy on the training

Welcome your Curly with open arms, a happy voice and lots of praise every time he comes to you.

leash. This time, catch him off-guard, while he's sniffing a leaf or watching a bird: "Albie, come!" You may have to pause for a split second after his name to be sure you have his attention. If the puppy shows any sign of confusion, give the leash a mild jerk and take a couple of steps backward. Do not repeat the command. In this case, you should say "Good come" as he reaches you.

That's the number-one rule of training. Each command word is given just once. Anything more is nagging. You'll also notice that all commands are one word only. Even when they are actually two words, you say them as one.

Never call the dog to come to you—with or without his name—if you are angry or intend to correct him for some misbehavior. When correcting the pup, you go to him. Your dog must always connect "Come" with something

pleasant and with your approval. If he learns that coming to you results in something good for him, then you can rely on his response.

Puppies, like children, have notoriously short attention spans, so don't overdo it with any of the training. Keep each lesson short. Break it up with a quick run around the yard or a ball toss, repeat the lesson and quit as soon as the pup gets it right. That way, you will always end with a "Good dog."

Life isn't perfect and neither are puppies. A time will come, often around ten months of age, when he'll become "selectively deaf" or choose to "forget" his name. He may respond by wagging his tail (and even seeming to smile at you) with a look that says "Make me!" Laugh, throw his favorite toy and skip the lesson you had planned. Pups will be pups!

COME AND GET IT!

The come command is your dog's safety signal. Until he is 99% perfect in responding, don't use the come command if you cannot enforce it. Practice on leash with treats or squeakers, or whenever the dog is running to you. Never call him to come to you if he is to be corrected for a misdemeanor. Reward the dog with a treat and happy praise whenever he comes to you.

THE HEEL EXERCISE

The second most important command to teach, after the come, is the heel. When you are walking your growing puppy, you need to be in control. Besides, it looks terrible to be pulled and yanked down the street, and it's not much fun either. Your eight- to ten-week-old puppy will probably follow you everywhere, but that's his natural instinct, not your control over the situation. However, any time he does follow you, you can say "Heel" and be ahead of the game, as he will learn to associate this command with the action of following you before you even begin teaching him to heel.

There is a very precise, almost military, procedure for teaching your dog to heel. As with all other obedience training, begin with the dog on your left side. He will be in a very nice sit and you will have the training leash across your chest. Hold the loop and folded leash in your right hand. Pick up the slack leash above the dog in your left hand and hold it loosely at your side. Step out on your left foot as you say "Heel." If the puppy does not move, give a gentle tug or pat your left leg to get him started. If he surges ahead of you, stop and pull him back gently until he is at your side. Tell him to sit and begin again.

Walk a few steps and stop while the puppy is correctly beside you. Tell him to sit and give mild verbal praise. (More enthusiastic praise will encourage him to think the lesson is over.) Repeat the lesson, increasing the

LET'S GO!

Many people use "Let's go" instead of "Heel" when teaching their dogs to behave on lead. It sounds more like fun! When beginning to teach the heel, whatever command you use, always step off on your left foot. That's the one next to the dog, who is on your left side, in case you've forgotten. Keep a loose leash. When the dog pulls ahead, stop, bring him back and begin again. Use treats to guide him around turns.

Heel training is necessary, since on-lead walks should be a part of your Curly's daily exercise. You take your dog for a walk, not the other way around!

tion. Give quiet, reassuring praise every time the leash goes slack and he's staying with you.

Staying and heeling can take a lot out of a dog, so provide playtime and free-running exercise to shake off the stress when the lessons are over. You don't want him to associate training with all work and no fun.

TAPERING OFF TIDBITS
Your dog has been watching you—and the hand that treats—throughout all of his lessons, and now it's time to break the treat

number of steps you take only as long as the dog is heeling nicely beside you. When you end the lesson, have him hold the sit, then give him the "Okay" to let him know that this is the end of the lesson. Praise him so that he knows he did a good job.

The cure for excessive pulling (a common problem) is to stop when the dog is no more than 2 or 3 feet ahead of you. Guide him back into position and begin again. With a really determined puller, try switching to a head collar. When used correctly, this will automatically turn the pup's head toward you so you can bring him back easily to the heel posi-

DON'T STRESS ME OUT
Your dog doesn't have to deal with paying the bills, the daily commute, PTA meetings and the like, but, believe it or not, there's a lot of stress in a dog's world. Stress can be caused by the owner's impatient demeanor and his angry or harsh corrections. If your dog cringes when you reach for his training collar, he's stressed. An older dog is sometimes stressed out when he goes to a new home. No matter what the cause, put off all training until he's over it. If he's going through a fear period—shying away from people, trembling when spoken to, avoiding eye contact or hiding under furniture—wait to resume training. Naturally you'd also postpone your lessons if the dog were sick, and the same goes for you. Show some compassion.

habit. Begin by giving him treats at the end of each lesson only. Then start to give a treat after the end of only some of the lessons. At the end of every lesson, as well as during the lessons, be consistent with the praise. Your pup now doesn't know whether he'll get a treat or not, but he should keep performing well just in case! Finally, you will stop giving treat rewards entirely. Save them for something brand-new that you want to teach him. Keep up the praise and you'll always have a "good dog."

OBEDIENCE CLASSES

The advantages of an obedience class are that your dog will have to learn amid the distractions of other people and dogs and that your mistakes will be quickly corrected by the trainer. Teaching your dog along with a qualified instructor and other handlers who may have more dog experience than you is another plus of the class environment. The instructor and other handlers can help you to find the most efficient way of teaching your dog a command or exercise. It's often easier to learn by other people's mistakes than your own. You will also learn all of the requirements for competitive obedience trials, in which you can earn titles and go on to advanced jumping and retrieving exercises, which are fun for many dogs. Obedience classes build the

MORE PRAISE, LESS FOOD

As you progress with your puppy's lessons, and the puppy is responding well, gradually begin to wean him off the treats by alternating the treats with times when you offer only verbal praise or a few pats on the dog's side. (Pats on the head are dominant actions, so he won't think they are meant to be praise.) Every lesson should end with the dog's performing the correct action for that session's command. When he gets it right and you withhold the treat, the praise can be as long and lavish as you like. The commands are one word only, but your verbal praise can use as many words as you want—don't skimp!

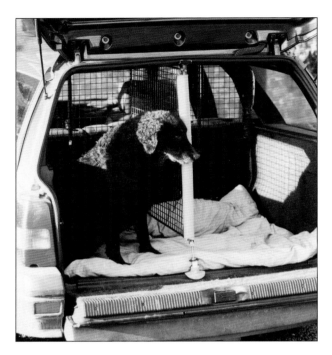

A well-trained Curly is easier to manage in every situation. Traveling with a trained dog can be a pleasure for everyone involved.

achieved obedience championships in both AKC and United Kennel Club (UKC) competition.

TRAINING FOR OTHER ACTIVITIES

Once your dog has basic obedience under his collar and is at least 12 months of age, you can enter the world of agility training. Dogs think agility is pure fun, like being turned loose in an amusement park full of obstacles! In addition to agility, there are hunting activities for sporting dogs, as well as tracking, which is open to all "nosey" dogs (which would include all dogs!). For those who like to volunteer, there is the wonderful feeling of owning a therapy dog and visiting hospices, nursing homes and veterans' homes to bring smiles, comfort and companionship to those who live there.

foundation needed for many other canine activities (in which we humans are allowed to participate, too!).

Although the Curly is not as precise at obedience as the Golden or the Labrador, the breed has become more popular in obedience competition and is capable of achieving a noteworthy degree of success in the obedience ring. Curlies learn quickly if proper training methods are applied. Because they have such an active mentality with a short attention span, they bore easily, which is a challenge for the average pet owner/trainer. However, in the United States several Curlies have

OKAY!
This is the signal that tells your dog that he can quit whatever he was doing. Use "Okay" to end a session on a correct response to a command. (Never end on an incorrect response.) Lots of praise follows. People use "Okay" a lot and it has other uses for dogs, too. Your dog is barking. You say, "Okay! Come!" "Okay" signals him to stop the barking activity and "Come" allows him to come to you for a "Good dog."

Field and gundog trials, along with working trials, are popular types of competition for Curlies, as these areas of the dog sport enable the breed to develop and utilize its instinctive abilities. These trials require higher levels of training, but are well suited to the breed and are a welcome outlet for the Curly's talent and energy.

Flyball is a team event in which the dogs run a series of jumps while carrying a ball over a specified course of hurdles. Several dogs comprise a flyball team, and the event is timed, making speed of the essence. The Curly is a natural for the sport, and more Curly owners are entering flyball competitions with their dogs.

Around the house, your Curly-Coated Retriever can be taught to do some simple chores. You might teach him to carry small household items or to fetch the morning newspaper. The kids can teach the dog all kinds of tricks, from playing hide-and-seek to balancing a biscuit on his nose. A family dog is what rounds out the family. Everything he does, including sitting at your feet and gazing lovingly at you, represents the bonus of owning a dog.

Most trainers use a dummy to begin retriever training. This will be your Curly's favorite exercise because it involves the breed's most natural ability. Throw the dummy (INSET) only when you have the dog's attention.

HEALTHCARE OF YOUR

CURLY-COATED RETRIEVER

By Lowell Ackerman DVM, DACVD

HEALTHCARE FOR A LIFETIME
When you own a dog, you become his healthcare advocate over his entire lifespan, as well as being the one to shoulder the financial burden of such care. Accordingly, it is worthwhile to focus on prevention rather than treatment, as you and your pet will both be happier.

Of course, the best place to have begun your program of preventive healthcare is with the initial purchase or adoption of your dog. There is no way of guaranteeing that your new furry friend is free of medical problems, but there are some things you can do to improve your odds. You certainly should have done adequate research into the Curly-Coated Retriever and have selected your puppy carefully rather than buying on impulse. Health issues aside, a large number of pet abandonment and relinquishment cases arise from a mismatch between pet needs and owner expectations. This is entirely preventable with appropriate planning and finding a good breeder.

Regarding healthcare issues specifically, it is very difficult to make blanket statements about where to acquire a problem-free pet, but, again, a reputable breeder is your best bet. In an ideal situation you have the opportunity to see both parents, get references from other owners of the breeder's pups and see genetic-testing documentation for several generations of the litter's ancestors. At the very least, you must thoroughly investigate the Curly-Coated Retriever and the problems inherent in the breed, as well as the genetic testing available to screen for those problems. Genetic testing offers some important benefits but is available for only a few disorders in a relatively small number of breeds and is not available for some of the most common genetic diseases, such as hip dysplasia, cataracts, epilepsy, cardiomyopathy, etc. This area of research is indeed exciting and increasingly important, and advances will continue to be made each year. In fact, recent research has shown that there is an equivalent dog gene for 75% of known human genes, so research done in either species is likely to benefit the other.

We've also discussed that evaluating the behavioral nature of your Curly-Coated Retriever and that of his immediate family members is an important part of the selection process that cannot be underestimated or overemphasized. It is sometimes difficult to evaluate temperament in puppies, because certain behavioral tendencies, such as some forms of aggression, may not be immediately evident. More dogs are euthanized each year for behavioral reasons than for all medical conditions combined, so it is critical to take temperament issues seriously. Start with a well-balanced, friendly companion and put the time and effort into proper socialization, and you will both be rewarded with a valued relationship for the life of the dog.

Assuming that you have started off with a pup from healthy, sound stock, you then become responsible for helping your veterinarian keep your pet healthy. Some crucial things happen before you even bring your puppy home. Parasite control typically begins at two weeks of age, and vaccinations typically begin at six to eight weeks of age. A pre-pubertal evaluation is typically scheduled for about six months of age. At this time, a dental evaluation is done (since the adult teeth are now in), heartworm prevention is started and neutering or spaying is most commonly done.

It is critical to commence regular dental care at home if you have not already done so. It may not sound very important, but most dogs have active periodontal disease by four years of age if they don't have their teeth cleaned regularly at home, not just at their veterinary exams. Dental problems lead to more than just bad "doggy breath." Gum disease can have very serious medical consequences. If you start brushing your dog's teeth and using antiseptic rinses from a young age, your dog will be accustomed to it and will not resist. The results will be healthy dentition, which your pet will need to enjoy a long, healthy life.

While most dogs are considered adults at a year of age, the Curly continues filling out for several years longer. Even individual dogs within each breed have different healthcare requirements, so work with your veterinarian to determine what will be needed and what your role should be. This doctor-client relationship is important, because as vaccination guide-

You must always supervise your Curly's outdoor time to make sure he is safe and that he doesn't get into anything that could endanger his health.

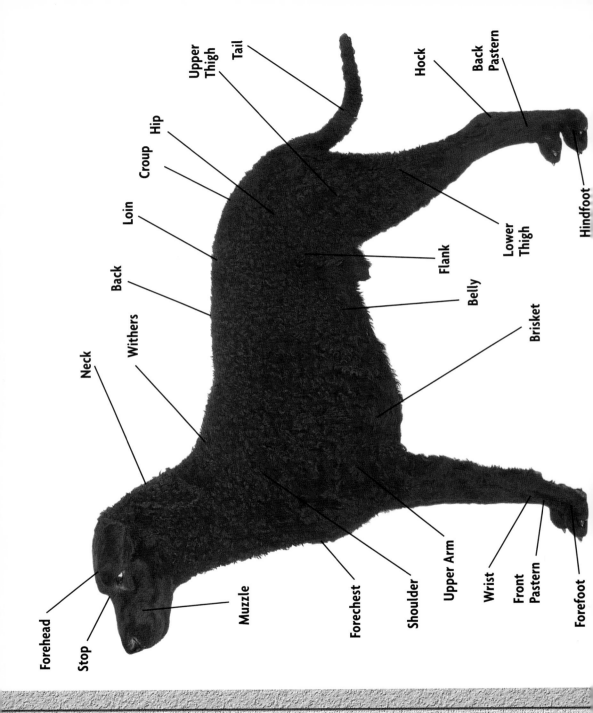

Upper Thigh

Tail

Hock

Back Pastern

Hip

Croup

Loin

Flank

Lower Thigh

Hindfoot

Back

Belly

Withers

Brisket

Neck

Upper Arm

Wrist

Front Pastern

Forefoot

Shoulder

Forechest

Muzzle

Forehead

Stop

PHYSICAL STRUCTURE OF THE CURLY-COATED RETRIEVER

lines change, there may not be an annual "vaccine visit" scheduled. You must make sure that you see your veterinarian at least annually, even if no vaccines are due, because this is the best opportunity to coordinate healthcare activities and to make sure that no medical issues creep by unaddressed.

When your Curly-Coated Retriever reaches three-quarters of his anticipated lifespan, he is

TAKING YOUR DOG'S TEMPERATURE

It is important to know how to take your dog's temperature at times when you think he may be ill. It's not the most enjoyable task, but it can be done without too much difficulty. It's easier with a helper, preferably someone with whom the dog is friendly, so that one of you can hold the dog while the other inserts the thermometer.

Before inserting the thermometer, coat the end with petroleum jelly. Insert the thermometer slowly and gently into the dog's rectum about one inch. Wait for the reading, about two minutes. Be sure to remove the thermometer carefully and clean it thoroughly after each use.

A dog's normal body temperature is between 100.5 and 102.5 degrees F. Immediate veterinary attention is required if the dog's temperature is below 99 or above 104 degrees F.

considered a "senior" and should receive some special care. In general, if you've been taking great care of your canine companion throughout his formative and adult years, the transition to senior status should be a smooth one. Age is not a disease, and as long as everything is functioning as it should, there is no reason why most of late adulthood should not be rewarding for both you and your pet. This is especially true if you have tended to the details, such as regular veterinary visits, proper dental care, excellent nutrition and management of bone and joint issues.

At this stage in your Curly-Coated Retriever's life, your veterinarian should want to schedule visits twice yearly, instead of once, to run some laboratory screenings, electrocardiograms and the like, and perhaps to change the diet to something more digestible. Catching problems early is the best way to manage them effectively. Treating the early stages of heart disease is so much easier than trying to intervene when there is more significant damage to the heart muscle. Similarly, managing the beginning of kidney problems is fairly routine if there is no significant kidney damage. Other problems, like cognitive dysfunction (similar to senility and Alzheimer's disease), cancer, diabetes and arthritis, are more common in older dogs, but all can

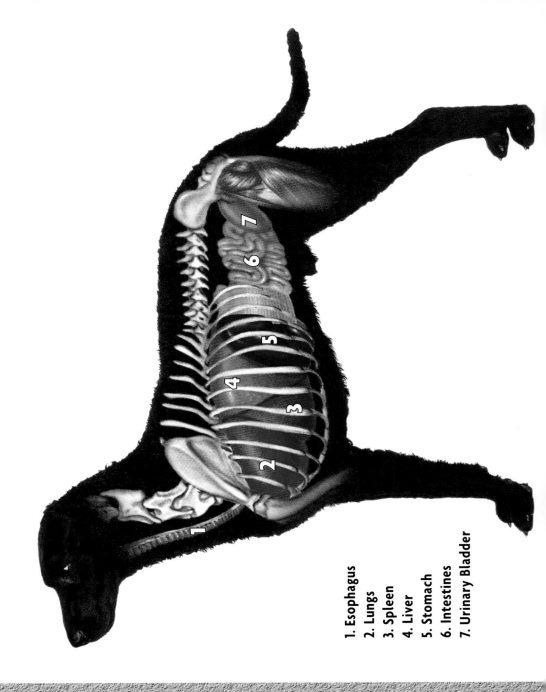

1. Esophagus
2. Lungs
3. Spleen
4. Liver
5. Stomach
6. Intestines
7. Urinary Bladder

INTERNAL ORGANS OF THE CURLY-COATED RETRIEVER

be treated to help the dog live as many happy, comfortable years as possible. Just as in people, medical management is more effective (and less expensive) when you catch things early.

SELECTING A VETERINARIAN
There is probably no more important decision that you will make regarding your pet's healthcare than the selection of his doctor. Your pet's veterinarian will be a pediatrician, family-practice physician and gerontologist, depending on the dog's life stage, and will be the individual who makes recommendations regarding issues such as when specialists need to be consulted, when diagnostic testing and/or therapeutic intervention is needed and when you will need to seek outside emergency and critical-care services. Your vet will act as your advocate and liaison throughout these processes.

Everyone has his own idea about what to look for in a vet, an individual who will play a big role in his dog's (and, of course, his own) life for many years to come. For some, it is the compassionate caregiver with whom they hope to develop a professional relationship to span the lives of their dogs and even their future pets. For others, they are seeking a clinician with keen diagnostic and therapeutic insight who can deliver state-of-the-art healthcare. Still others need a veterinary facility that is open

YOUR DOG NEEDS TO VISIT THE VET IF:
- He has ingested a toxin such as antifreeze or a toxic plant; in these cases, administer first aid and call the vet right away
- His teeth are discolored, loose or missing or he has sores or other signs of infection or abnormality in the mouth
- He has been vomiting, has had diarrhea or has been constipated for over 24 hours; call immediately if you notice blood
- He has refused food for over 24 hours
- His eating habits, water intake or toilet habits have noticeably changed; if you have noticed weight gain or weight loss
- He shows symptoms of bloat, which requires *immediate* attention
- He is salivating excessively
- He has a lump in his throat
- He has a lump or bumps anywhere on the body
- He is very lethargic
- He appears to be in pain or otherwise has trouble chewing or swallowing
- His skin loses elasticity

Of course, there will be other instances in which a visit to the vet is necessary; these are just some of the signs that could be indicative of serious problems that need to be caught as early as possible.

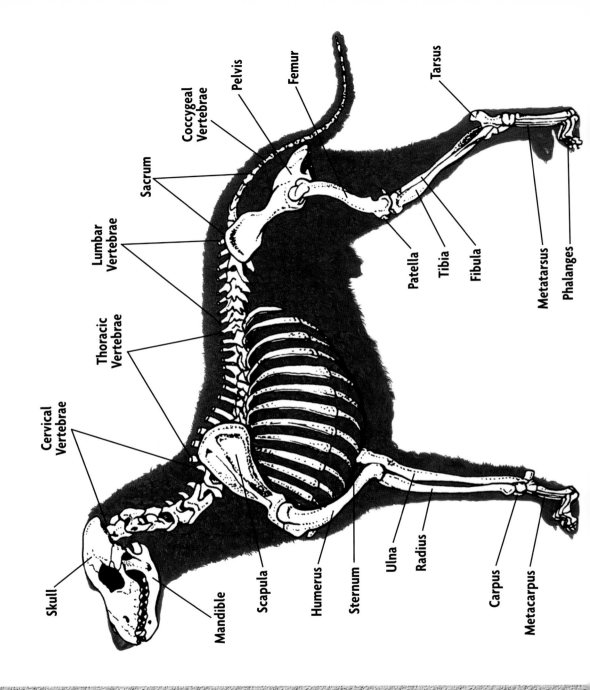

Coccygeal Vertebrae
Pelvis
Femur
Tarsus
Sacrum
Lumbar Vertebrae
Patella
Tibia
Fibula
Metatarsus
Phalanges
Thoracic Vertebrae
Cervical Vertebrae
Skull
Mandible
Scapula
Humerus
Sternum
Ulna
Radius
Carpus
Metacarpus

SKELETAL STRUCTURE OF THE CURLY-COATED RETRIEVER

evenings and weekends, is in close proximity or provides mobile veterinary services to accommodate their schedules; these people may not much mind that their dogs might see different veterinarians on each visit. Just as we have different reasons for selecting our own healthcare professionals (e.g., covered by insurance plan, expert in field, convenient location, etc.), we should not expect that there is a one-size-fits-all recommendation for selecting a veterinarian and veterinary practice. The best advice is to be honest in your assessment of what you expect from a veterinary practice and to conscientiously research the options in your area. You will quickly appreciate that not all veterinary practices are the same, and you will be happiest with one that truly meets your needs.

DENTAL WARNING SIGNS

A veterinary dental exam is necessary if you notice one or any combination of the following in your dog:
- Broken, loose or missing teeth
- Loss of appetite (which could be due to mouth pain or illness caused by infection)
- Gum abnormalities, including redness, swelling and bleeding
- Drooling, with or without blood
- Yellowing of the teeth or gumline, indicating tartar
- Bad breath

There is another point to be considered in the selection of veterinary services. Not that long ago, a single veterinarian would attempt to manage all medical and surgical issues as they arose. That was often problematic, because veterinarians are trained in many species and many diseases, and it was just impossible for general veterinary practitioners to be experts in every species, every breed, every field and every ailment. However, just as in the human healthcare fields, specialization has allowed general practitioners to concentrate on primary healthcare delivery, especially wellness and the prevention of infectious diseases, and to utilize a network of specialists to assist in the management of conditions that require specific expertise and experience. Thus there are now many types of veterinary specialists, including dermatologists, cardiologists, ophthalmologists, surgeons, internists, oncologists, neurologists, behaviorists, criticalists and others to help primary-care veterinarians deal with complicated medical challenges. In most cases, specialists see cases referred by primary-care veterinarians, make diagnoses and set up management plans. From there, the animals' ongoing care is returned to their primary-care veterinarians. This important team approach to your pet's medical-care needs has provided opportunities for advanced care and an unparalleled level of quality to be delivered.

With all of the opportunities for your Curly-Coated Retriever to receive high-quality veterinary medical care, there is another topic that needs to be addressed at the same time—cost. It's been said that you can have excellent healthcare or inexpensive healthcare, but never both; this is as true in veterinary medicine as it is in human medicine. While veterinary costs are a fraction of what the same services cost in the human health-care arena, it is still difficult to deal with unanticipated medical costs, especially since they can easily creep into hundreds or even thousands of dollars if specialists or emergency services become involved. However, there are ways of managing these risks. The easiest is to buy pet health insurance and realize that its foremost purpose is not to cover routine healthcare visits but rather to serve as an umbrella for those rainy days when your pet needs medical care and you don't want to worry about whether or not you can afford that care.

Pet-insurance policies are very cost-effective (and very inexpensive by human health-insurance standards), but make sure that you buy the policy long before you intend to use it (preferably starting in puppyhood, because coverage will exclude pre-existing conditions) and that you are actually buying an indemnity insurance plan from an insurance company that is regulated by your state or province. Many insurance policy look-alikes are actually discount clubs that are redeemable only at specific locations and for specific services. An indemnity plan covers your pet at almost all veterinary, specialty and emergency practices and is an excellent way to manage your pet's ongoing healthcare needs.

VACCINATIONS AND INFECTIOUS DISEASES

There has never been an easier time to prevent a variety of infectious diseases in your dog, but the advances we've made in veterinary medicine come with a price— choice. Now while it may seem that this choice is a good thing (and it is), it also has never been more difficult for the pet owner (or the vet) to make an informed decision about the best way to protect pets through vaccination.

Years ago, it was just accepted that puppies got a starter series of vaccinations and then annual "boosters" throughout their lives to keep them protected. As more and more vaccines became available, consumers wanted the convenience of having all of that protection in a single injection. The result was "multivalent" vaccines that crammed a lot of protection into a single syringe. The manufacturers' recommendations were to give the vaccines annually, and this was a simple enough protocol to follow. However, as veterinary medicine has become more sophisticated and we have started looking more at healthcare quandaries rather than convenience, it became necessary to reevaluate the situation and deal with some tough questions. It is important to realize that whether or not to use a particular vaccine depends on the risk of contracting the disease against which it protects, the severity of the disease if it is contracted, the duration of immunity provided by the vaccine, the safety of the product and the needs of the individual animal. In a very general sense, rabies, distemper, hepatitis and parvovirus are considered core vaccine needs, while parainfluenza, *Bordetella bronchiseptica*, leptospirosis, coronavirus and borreliosis (Lyme disease) are considered non-core needs and best reserved for animals that demonstrate reasonable risk of contracting the diseases.

NEUTERING/SPAYING

Sterilization procedures (neutering for males/spaying for females) are meant to accomplish several purposes. While the underlying premise is to address the risk of pet overpopulation, there are also some medical and behavioral benefits to the surgeries. For females, spaying prior to the first estrus (heat cycle) leads to a marked reduction in the risk of mammary cancer and other serious female health problems. There also will be no manifestations of "heat" to attract male dogs and no bleeding in the house. For males, there is prevention of testicular cancer and a reduction in the risk of prostate problems. In both sexes there may be some limited reduction in aggressive behaviors toward other dogs and some diminishing of urine marking, roaming and mounting.

While neutering and spaying do indeed prevent animals from contributing to pet overpopulation, even no-cost and low-cost neutering options have not eliminated the problem. Perhaps one of the main reasons for this is that individuals that intentionally breed their dogs and those that allow their animals to run at large are the main causes of unwanted offspring. Also, animals in shelters are often there because they were abandoned or relinquished, not because they came from unplanned matings. Neutering/ spaying is important, but it should be considered in the context of the real causes of animals' ending up in shelters and eventually being euthanized.

One of the important considerations regarding neutering is that it is a surgical procedure. This sometimes gets lost in discussions of low-cost procedures and commodi-

COMMON INFECTIOUS DISEASES

Let's discuss some of the diseases that create the need for vaccination in the first place. Following are the major canine infectious diseases and a simple explanation of each.

Rabies: A devastating viral disease that can be fatal in dogs and people. In fact, vaccination of dogs and cats is an important public-health measure to create a resistant animal buffer population to protect people from contracting the disease. Vaccination schedules are determined on a government level and are not optional for pet owners; rabies vaccination is required by law in all 50 states.

Parvovirus: A severe, potentially life-threatening disease that is easily transmitted between dogs. There are four strains of the virus, but it is believed that there is significant "cross-protection" between strains that may be included in individual vaccines.

Distemper: A potentially severe and life-threatening disease with a relatively high risk of exposure, especially in certain regions. In very high-risk distemper environments, young pups may be vaccinated with human measles vaccine, a related virus that offers cross-protection when administered at four to ten weeks of age.

Hepatitis: Caused by canine adenovirus type 1 (CAV-1), but since vaccination with the causative virus has a higher rate of adverse effects, cross-protection is derived from the use of adenovirus type 2 (CAV-2), a cause of respiratory disease and one of the potential causes of canine cough. Vaccination with CAV-2 provides long-term immunity against hepatitis, but relatively less protection against respiratory infection.

Canine cough: Also called tracheobronchitis, actually a fairly complicated result of viral and bacterial offenders; therefore, even with vaccination, protection is incomplete. Wherever dogs congregate, canine cough will likely be spread among them. Intranasal vaccination with *Bordetella* and parainfluenza is the best safeguard, but the duration of immunity does not appear to be very long, typically a year at most. These are non-core vaccines, but vaccination is sometimes mandated by boarding kennels, obedience classes, dog shows and other places where dogs congregate to try to minimize spread of infection.

Leptospirosis: A potentially fatal disease that is more common in some geographic regions. It is capable of being spread to humans. The disease varies with the individual "serovar," or strain, of *Leptospira* involved. Since there does not appear to be much cross-protection between serovars, protection is only as good as the likelihood that the serovar in the vaccine is the same as the one in the pet's local environment. Problems with *Leptospira* vaccines are that protection does not last very long, side effects are not uncommon and a large percentage of dogs (perhaps 30%) may not respond to vaccination.

Borrelia burgdorferi: The cause of Lyme disease, the risk of which varies with the geographic area in which the pet lives and travels. Lyme disease is spread by deer ticks in the eastern US and western black-legged ticks in the western part of the country, and the risk of exposure is high in some regions. Lameness, fever and inappetence are most commonly seen in affected dogs. The extent of protection from the vaccine has not been conclusively demonstrated.

Coronavirus: This disease has a high risk of exposure, especially in areas where dogs congregate, but it typically causes only mild to moderate digestive upset (diarrhea, vomiting, etc.). Vaccines are available, but the duration of protection is believed to be relatively short and the effectiveness of the vaccine in preventing infection is considered low.

There are many other vaccinations available, including those for *Giardia* and canine adenovirus-1. While there may be some specific indications for their use, and local risk factors to be considered, they are not widely recommended for most dogs.

tization of the process. In females, spaying is specifically referred to as an ovariohysterectomy. In this procedure, a midline incision is made in the abdomen and the entire uterus and both ovaries are surgically removed. While this is a major invasive surgical procedure, it usually has few complications because it is typically performed on healthy young animals. However, it is major surgery, as any woman who has had a hysterectomy will attest.

In males, neutering has traditionally referred to castration, which involves the surgical removal of both testicles. While still a significant piece of surgery, there is not the abdominal exposure that is required in the female surgery. In addition, there is now a chemical sterilization option, in which a solution is injected into each testicle, leading to atrophy of the sperm-producing cells. This can typically be done under sedation rather than full anesthesia. This is a relatively new approach, and there are no long-term clinical studies yet available.

Neutering/spaying is typically done around six months of age at most veterinary hospitals, although techniques have been pioneered to perform the procedures in animals as young as eight weeks of age. In general, the surgeries on the very young animals are done for the specific reason of sterilizing them before they go to their new homes.

This is done in some shelter hospitals for assurance that the animals will definitely not produce any pups. Otherwise, these organizations need to rely on owners to comply with their wishes to have the animals "altered" at a later date, something that does not always happen.

PROBLEM: AND THAT STARTS WITH "P"

Urinary tract problems more commonly affect female dogs, especially those who have been spayed. The first sign that a urinary tract problem exists usually is a strong odor from the urine or an unusual color. Blood in the urine, known as hematuria, is another sign of an infection, related to cystitis, a bladder infection, bladder cancer or a blood-clotting disorder. Urinary tract problems can also be signaled by the dog's straining while urinating, experiencing pain during urination and genital discharge as well as excessive water intake and urination.

Excessive drinking, in and of itself, does not indicate a urinary tract problem. A dog who is drinking more than normal may have a kidney or liver problem, a hormonal disorder or diabetes mellitus. Behaviorists report a disorder known as psychogenic polydipsia, which manifests itself in excessive drinking and urination. If you notice your dog drinking much more than normal, get to the vet.

A scanning electron micrograph of a dog flea, *Ctenocephalides canis*, on dog hair.

EXTERNAL PARASITES

FLEAS

Fleas have been around for millions of years and, while we have better tools now for controlling them than at any time in the past, there still is little chance that they will end up on an endangered species list. Actually, they are very well adapted to living on our pets, and they continue to adapt as we make advances.

The female flea can consume 15 times her weight in blood during active reproduction and can lay as many as 40 eggs a day. These eggs are very resistant to the effects of insecticides. They hatch into larvae, which then mature and spin cocoons. The immature fleas reside in this pupal stage until the time is right for feeding. This pupal stage is also very resistant to the effects of insecticides, and pupae can last in the environment without feeding for many months. Newly emergent fleas are attracted to animals by the warmth of the animals' bodies, movement and exhaled carbon dioxide. However, when they first emerge from their cocoons, they orient towards light; thus when an animal passes between a flea and the light source, casting a shadow, the flea pounces and starts to feed. If the animal turns out to be a dog or cat, the reproductive cycle continues. If the flea lands on another type of animal, including a person, the flea will bite but will then look for a more appropriate host. An emerging adult flea can survive without feeding for up to 12 months but, once it tastes blood, it can survive off its host for only 3 to 4 days.

It was once thought that fleas spend most of their lives in the environment, but we now know that fleas won't willingly jump off a dog unless leaping to another dog or when physically removed by brushing, bathing or other manipulation. Flea eggs, on the other hand, are shiny and smooth, and they roll off the animal and into the environment. The eggs, larvae and pupae then exist in the environment, but once the adult finds a susceptible animal, it's home sweet home until the flea is forced to seek refuge elsewhere.

Since adult fleas live on the animal and immature forms survive in the environment, a successful treatment plan must address all stages of the flea life cycle. There are now several safe and effective flea-control products that can be applied on a monthly

> ## FLEA PREVENTION FOR YOUR DOG
>
> - Discuss with your veterinarian the safest product to protect your dog, likely in the form of a monthly tablet or a liquid preparation placed on the back of the dog's neck.
> - For dogs suffering from flea-bite dermatitis, a shampoo or topical insecticide treatment is required.
> - Your lawn and property should be sprayed with an insecticide designed to kill fleas and ticks that lurk outdoors.
> - Using a flea comb, check the dog's coat regularly for any signs of parasites.
> - Practice good housekeeping. Vacuum floors, carpets and furniture regularly, especially in the areas that the dog frequents, and wash the dog's bedding weekly.
> - Follow up house-cleaning with carpet shampoos and sprays to rid the house of fleas at all stages of development. Insect growth regulators are the safest option.

basis. These include fipronil, imidacloprid, selamectin and permethrin (found in several formulations). Most of these products have significant flea-killing rates within 24 hours. However, none of them will control the immature forms in the environment. To accomplish this, there are a variety of insect growth regulators that can be sprayed into

THE FLEA'S LIFE CYCLE

What came first, the flea or the egg? This age-old mystery is more difficult to comprehend than the actual cycle of the flea. Fleas usually live only about four months. A female can lay 2,000 eggs in her lifetime.

Egg

After ten days of rolling around your carpet or under your furniture, the eggs hatch into larvae, which feed on various and sundry debris. In days or

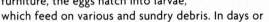

Larva

months, depending on the climate, the larvae spin cocoons and develop into the pupal or nymph stage, which quickly develop into fleas.

Pupa

These immature fleas must locate a host within 10 to 14 days or they will die. Only about 1% of the flea population exist as adult fleas, while the other 99% exist as eggs, larvae or pupae.

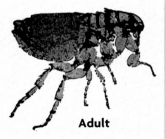

Adult

Photo by Carolina Biological Supply Co.

KILL FLEAS THE NATURAL WAY

If you choose not to go the route of conventional medication, there are some natural ways to ward off fleas:

- Dust your dog with a natural flea powder, composed of such herbal goodies as rosemary, wormwood, pennyroyal, citronella, rue, tobacco powder and eucalyptus.
- Apply diatomaceous earth, the fossilized remains of single-cell algae, to your carpets, furniture and pet's bedding. Even though it's not good for dogs, it's even worse for fleas, which will dry up swiftly and die.
- Brush your dog frequently, give him adequate exercise and let him fast occasionally. All of these activities strengthen the dog's immune system and make him more resistant to disease and parasites.
- Bathe your dog with a capful of pennyroyal or eucalyptus oil.
- Feed a natural diet, free of additives and preservatives. Add a little fresh garlic and brewer's yeast to the dog's morning portion, as these items have flea-repelling properties.

the environment (e.g., pyriproxyfen, methoprene, fenoxycarb) as well as insect development inhibitors such as lufenuron that can be administered. These compounds have no effect on adult fleas, but they stop immature forms from developing into adults. In years gone by, we relied heavily on toxic insecticides (such as organophosphates, organochlorines and carbamates) to manage the flea problem, but today's options are not only much safer to use on our pets but also safer for the environment.

TICKS

Ticks are members of the spider class (arachnids) and are blood-sucking parasites capable of transmitting a variety of diseases, including Lyme disease, ehrlichiosis, babesiosis and Rocky Mountain spotted fever. It's easy to see ticks on your own skin, but it is more of a challenge when your furry companion is affected. Whenever you happen to be planning a stroll in a tick-infested area (especially forests, grassy or wooded areas or parks) be prepared to do a thorough inspection of your dog afterward to search for ticks. Ticks can be tricky, so make sure you spend time looking in the ears, between the toes and everywhere else where a tick might hide. Ticks need to be attached for 24–72 hours before they transmit most of the diseases that they carry, so you do have a window of opportunity for some preventive intervention.

S. E. M. BY PHOTOTAKE.

A TICKING BOMB

There is nothing good about a tick's harpooning his nose into your dog's skin. Among the diseases caused by ticks are Rocky Mountain spotted fever, canine ehrlichiosis, canine babesiosis, canine hepatozoonosis and Lyme disease. If a dog is allergic to the saliva of a female wood tick, he can develop tick paralysis.

Female ticks live to eat and breed. They can lay between 4,000 and 5,000 eggs and they die soon after. Males, on the other hand, live only to mate with the females and continue the process as long as they are able. Most ticks live on multiple hosts before parasitizing dogs. The immature forms typically reside on grass and shrubs, waiting for susceptible animals to walk by. The larvae and nymph stages typically feed on wildlife.

If only a few ticks are present on a dog, they can be plucked out, but it is important to remove the entire head and mouthparts,

A scanning electron micrograph of the head of a female deer tick, *Ixodes dammini*, a parasitic tick that carries Lyme disease.

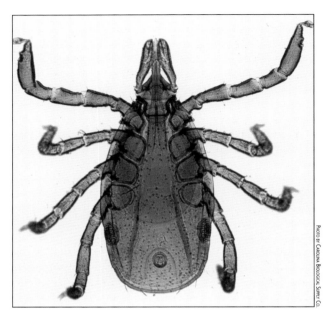

PHOTO BY CAROLINA BIOLOGICAL SUPPLY CO.

Deer tick,
Ixodes dammini.

of in a container of alcohol or household bleach.

Some of the newer flea products, specifically those with fipronil, selamectin and permethrin, have effect against some, but not all, species of tick. Flea collars containing appropriate pesticides (e.g., propoxur, chlorfenvinphos) can aid in tick control. In most areas, such collars should be placed on animals in March, at the beginning of the tick season, and changed regularly. Leaving the collar on when the pesticide level is waning invites the development of resistance. Amitraz collars are also good for tick control, and the active ingredient does not interfere with other flea-control products. The ingredient helps prevent the attachment of ticks to the skin and will cause those ticks already on the skin to detach themselves.

which may be deeply embedded in the skin. This is best accomplished with forceps designed especially for this purpose; fingers can be used but should be protected with rubber gloves, plastic wrap or at least a paper towel. The tick should be grasped as closely as possible to the animal's skin and should be pulled upward with steady, even pressure. Do not squeeze, crush or puncture the body of the tick or you risk exposure to any disease carried by that tick. Once the ticks have been removed, the sites of attachment should be disinfected. Your hands should then be washed with soap and water to further minimize risk of contagion. The tick should be disposed

TICK CONTROL

Removal of underbrush and leaf litter and the thinning of trees in areas where tick control is desired are recommended. These actions remove the cover and food sources for small animals that serve as hosts for ticks. With continued mowing of grasses in these areas, the probability of ticks' surviving is further reduced. A variety of insecticide ingredients (e.g., resmethrin, carbaryl, permethrin, chlorpyrifos, dioxathion and allethrin) are registered for tick control around the home.

MITES

Mites are tiny arachnid parasites that parasitize the skin of dogs. Skin diseases caused by mites are referred to as "mange," and there are many different forms seen in dogs. These forms are very different from one another, each one warranting an individual description.

Sarcoptic mange, or scabies, is one of the itchiest conditions that affects dogs. The microscopic *Sarcoptes* mites burrow into the superficial layers of the skin and can drive dogs crazy with itchiness. They are also communicable to people, although they can't complete their reproductive cycle on people. In addition to being tiny, the mites also are often difficult to find when trying to make a diagnosis. Skin scrapings from multiple areas are examined microscopically but, even then, sometimes the mites cannot be found.

Fortunately, scabies is relatively easy to treat, and there are a variety of products that will successfully kill the mites. Since the mites can't live in the environment for very long without feeding, a complete cure is usually possible within four to eight weeks.

Cheyletiellosis is caused by a relatively large mite, which sometimes can be seen even without a microscope. Often referred to as "walking dandruff," this also causes itching, but not usually as profound as with scabies. While *Cheyletiella* mites can survive somewhat longer

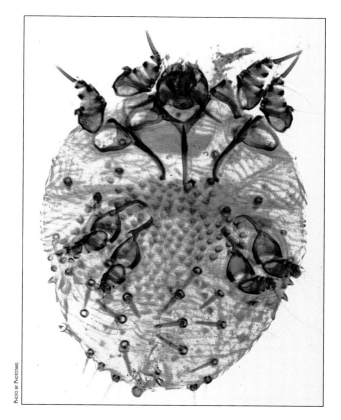

PHOTO BY PHOTOTAKE.

Sarcoptes scabiei, commonly known as the "itch mite."

in the environment than scabies mites, they too are relatively easy to treat, being responsive to not only the medications used to treat scabies but also often to flea-control products.

Otodectes cynotis is the canine ear mite and is one of the more common causes of mange, especially in young dogs in shelters or pet stores. That's because the mites are typically present in large numbers and are quickly spread to nearby animals. The mites rarely do much harm but can be difficult

Micrograph of a dog louse, *Heterodoxus spiniger*. Female lice attach their eggs to the hairs of the dog. As the eggs hatch, the larval lice bite and feed on the blood. Lice can also feed on dead skin and hair. This feeding activity can cause hair loss and skin problems.

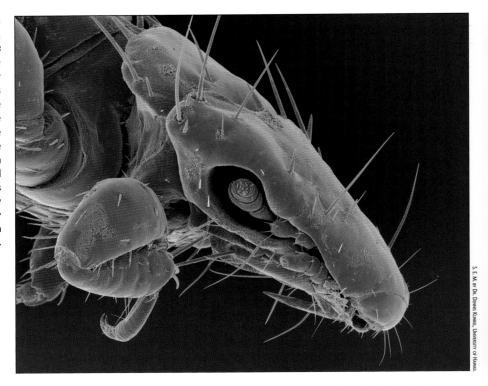

to eradicate if the treatment regimen is not comprehensive. While many try to treat the condition with ear drops only, this is the most common cause of treatment failure. Ear drops cause the mites to simply move out of the ears and as far away as possible (usually to the base of the tail) until the insecticide levels in the ears drop to an acceptable level—then it's back to business as usual! The successful treatment of ear mites requires treating all animals in the household with a systemic insecticide, such as selamectin, or a combination of miticidal ear drops combined with whole-body flea-control preparations.

Demodicosis, sometimes referred to as red mange, can be one of the most difficult forms of mange to treat. Part of the problem has to do with the fact that the mites live in the hair follicles and they are relatively well shielded from topical and systemic products. The main issue, however, is that demodectic mange typically results only when there is some underlying process interfering with the dog's immune system.

Since *Demodex* mites are normal residents of the skin of

mammals, including humans, there is usually a mite population explosion only when the immune system fails to keep the number of mites in check. In young animals, the immune deficit may be transient or may reflect an actual inherited immune problem. In older animals, demodicosis is usually seen only when there is another disease hampering the immune system, such as diabetes, cancer, thyroid problems or the use of immune-suppressing drugs. Accordingly, treatment involves not only trying to kill the mange mites but also discerning what is interfering with immune function and correcting it if possible.

Chiggers represent several different species of mite that don't parasitize dogs specifically, but do latch on to passersby and can cause irritation. The problem is most prevalent in wooded areas in the late summer and fall. Treatment is not difficult, as the mites do not complete their life cycle on dogs and are susceptible to a variety of miticidal products.

MOSQUITOES

Mosquitoes have long been known to transmit a variety of diseases to people, as well as just being biting pests during warm weather. They also pose a real risk to pets. Not only do they carry deadly heartworms but

recently there also has been much concern over their involvement with West Nile virus. While we can avoid heartworm with the use of preventive medications, there are no such preventives for West Nile virus. The only method of prevention in endemic areas is active mosquito control. Fortunately, most dogs that have been exposed to the virus only developed flu-like symptoms and, to date, there have not been the large number of reported deaths in canines as seen in some other species.

Illustration of Demodex folliculoram.

ILLUSTRATION BY PHOTOTAKE.

MOSQUITO REPELLENT

Low concentrations of DEET (less than 10%), found in many human mosquito repellents, have been safely used on dogs but, in these concentrations, probably give only about two hours of protection. DEET may be safe in these small concentrations, but since it is not licensed for use on dogs, there is no research proving its safety for dogs. Products containing permethrin give the longest-lasting protection, perhaps two to four weeks. As DEET is not licensed for use on dogs, and both DEET and permethrin can be quite toxic to cats, appropriate care should be exercised. Other products, such as those containing oil of citronella, also have some mosquito-repellent activity, but typically have a relatively short duration of action.

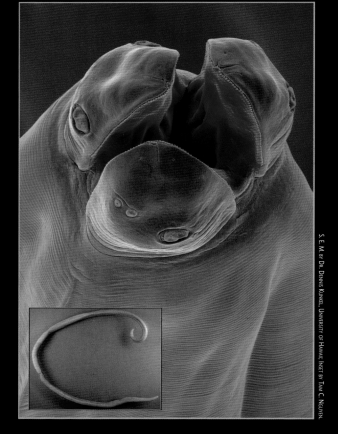

ASCARID DANGERS

The most commonly encountered worms in dogs are roundworms known as ascarids. *Toxascaris leonine* and *Toxocara canis* are the two species that infect dogs. Subsisting in the dog's stomach and intestines, adult round-worms can grow to 7 inches in length and adult females can lay in excess of 200,000 eggs in a single day.

In humans, visceral larval migrans affects people who have ingested eggs of *Toxocara canis*, which frequently contaminates children's sandboxes, beaches and park grounds. The round-worms reside in the human's stomach and intestines, as they would in a dog's, but do not mature. Instead, they find their way to the liver, lungs and skin, or even to the heart or kidneys in severe cases. Deworming puppies is critical in preventing the infection in humans, and young children should never handle nursing pups who have not been dewormed.

The ascarid roundworm *Toxocara canis*, showing the mouth with three lips. INSET: Photomicrograph of the roundworm *Ascaris lumbricoides*.

INTERNAL PARASITES: WORMS

ASCARIDS

Ascarids are intestinal round-worms that rarely cause severe disease in dogs. Nonetheless, they are of major public health significance because they can be transferred to people. Sadly, it is children who are most commonly affected by the parasite, probably from inadvertently ingesting ascarid-contaminated soil. In fact, many yards and children's sand-boxes contain appreciable numbers of ascarid eggs. So, while ascarids don't bite dogs or latch onto their intestines to suck blood, they do cause some nasty medical conditions in children and are best eradicated from our furry friends. Because pups can start passing ascarid eggs by three weeks of age, most parasite-control programs begin at two weeks of age and are repeated every two weeks until pups are eight weeks old. It is important to

S. E. M. BY DR. DENNIS KUNKEL, UNIVERSITY OF HAWAII.

realize that bitches can pass ascarids to their pups even if they test negative prior to whelping. Accordingly, bitches are best treated at the same time as the pups.

HOOKWORMS

Unlike ascarids, hookworms do latch onto a dog's intestinal tract and can cause significant loss of blood and protein. Similar to ascarids, hookworms can be transmitted to humans, where they cause a condition known as cutaneous larval migrans. Dogs can become infected either by consuming the infective larvae or by the larvae's penetrating the skin directly. People most often get infected when they are lying on the ground (such as on a beach) and the larvae penetrate the skin. Yes, the larvae can penetrate through a beach blanket. Hookworms are typically susceptible to the same medications used to treat ascarids.

The hookworm *Ancylostoma caninum* infests the intestines of dogs. INSET: Note the row of hooks at the posterior end, used to anchor the worm to the intestinal wall.

WHIPWORMS

Whipworms latch onto the lower aspects of the dog's colon and can cause cramping and diarrhea. Eggs do not start to appear in the dog's feces until about three months after the dog was infected. This worm has a peculiar life cycle, which makes it more difficult to control than ascarids or hookworms. The good thing is that whipworms rarely are transferred to people.

Some of the medications used to treat ascarids and hookworms are also effective against whipworms, but, in general, a separate treatment protocol is needed. Since most of the medications are effective against the adults but not the eggs or larvae, treatment is typically repeated in three weeks, and then often in three

> ## WORM-CONTROL GUIDELINES
> - Practice sanitary habits with your dog and home.
> - Clean up after your dog and don't let him sniff or eat other dogs' droppings.
> - Control insects and fleas in the dog's environment. Fleas, lice, cockroaches, beetles, mice and rats can act as hosts for various worms.
> - Prevent dogs from eating uncooked meat, raw poultry and dead animals.
> - Keep dogs and children from playing in sand and soil.
> - Kennel dogs on cement or gravel; avoid dirt runs.
> - Administer heartworm preventives regularly.
> - Have your vet examine your dog's stools at your annual visits.
> - Select a boarding kennel carefully so as to avoid contamination from other dogs or an unsanitary environment.
> - Prevent dogs from roaming. Obey local leash laws.

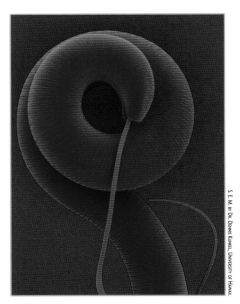

Adult whipworm, *Trichuris* sp., an intestinal parasite.

S.E.M. BY DR. DENNIS KUNKEL, UNIVERSITY OF HAWAII.

months as well. Unfortunately, since dogs don't develop resistance to whipworms, it is difficult to prevent them from getting reinfected if they visit soil contaminated with whipworm eggs.

TAPEWORMS

There are many different species of tapeworm that affect dogs, but *Dipylidium caninum* is probably the most common and is spread by fleas. Flea larvae feed on organic debris and tapeworm eggs in the environment and, when a dog chews at himself and manages to ingest fleas, he might get a dose of tapeworm at the same time. The tapeworm then develops further in the intestine of the dog.

The tapeworm itself, which is a parasitic flatworm that latches onto the intestinal wall, is composed of numerous segments. When the segments break off into the intestine (as proglottids), they may accumulate around the rectum like grains of rice. While this tapeworm is disgusting in its behavior, it is not directly communicable to humans (although humans can also get infected by swallowing fleas).

A much more dangerous flatworm is *Echinococcus multilocularis*, which is typically found in foxes, coyotes and wolves. The eggs are passed in the feces and infect rodents, and, when dogs eat the rodents, the dogs can be infected by thousands of adult tapeworms. While the parasites don't cause many problems in dogs, this is considered the most lethal worm infection that people can get. Take appropriate precautions if you live in an area in which these tapeworms are found. Do not use mulch that may contain feces of dogs, cats or wildlife, and discourage your pets from hunting

wildlife. Treat these tapeworm infections aggressively in pets, because if humans get infected, approximately half die.

HEARTWORMS

Heartworm disease is caused by the parasite *Dirofilaria immitis* and is seen in dogs around the world. A member of the roundworm group, it is spread between dogs by the bite of an infected mosquito. The mosquito injects infective larvae into the dog's skin with its bite, and these larvae develop under the skin for a period of time before making their way to the heart. There they develop into adults, which grow and create blockages of the heart, lungs and major blood vessels there. They also start producing offspring (microfilariae),

A dog tapeworm proglottid (body segment).

The dog tapeworm *Taenia pisiformis*.

S. E. M. BY DR. DENNIS KUNKEL, UNIVERSITY OF HAWAII.

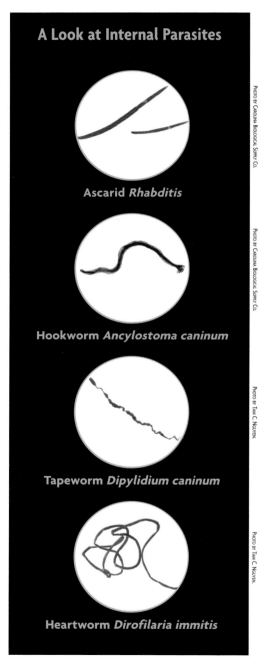

A Look at Internal Parasites

Ascarid *Rhabditis*

Hookworm *Ancylostoma caninum*

Tapeworm *Dipylidium caninum*

Heartworm *Dirofilaria immitis*

and these microfilariae circulate in the bloodstream, waiting to hitch a ride when the next mosquito bites. Once in the mosquito, the microfilariae develop into infective larvae and the entire process is repeated.

When dogs get infected with heartworm, over time they tend to develop symptoms associated with heart disease, such as coughing, exercise intolerance and potentially many other manifestations. Diagnosis is confirmed by either seeing the microfilariae themselves in blood samples or using immunologic tests (antigen testing) to identify the presence of adult heartworms. Since antigen tests measure the presence of adult heartworms and microfilarial tests measure offspring produced by adults, neither are positive until six to seven months after the initial infection. However, the beginning of damage can occur by fifth-stage larvae as early as three months after infection. Thus it is possible for dogs to be harboring problem-causing larvae for up to three months before either type of test would identify an infection.

The good news is that there are great protocols available for preventing heartworm in dogs. Testing is critical in the process, and it is important to understand the benefits as well as the limitations of such testing. All dogs six months of age or older that have not been on continuous heartworm-preventive medication should be

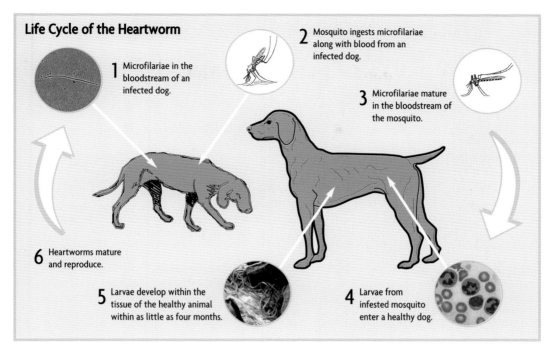

Life Cycle of the Heartworm

1 Microfilariae in the bloodstream of an infected dog.

2 Mosquito ingests microfilariae along with blood from an infected dog.

3 Microfilariae mature in the bloodstream of the mosquito.

4 Larvae from infested mosquito enter a healthy dog.

5 Larvae develop within the tissue of the healthy animal within as little as four months.

6 Heartworms mature and reproduce.

screened with microfilarial or anti-gen tests. For dogs receiving preventive medication, periodic antigen testing helps assess the effectiveness of the preventives. The American Heartworm Society guidelines suggest that annual retesting may not be necessary when owners have absolutely provided continuous heartworm prevention. Retesting on a two- to three-year interval may be sufficient in these cases. However, your veterinarian will likely have specific guidelines under which heartworm preventives will be prescribed, and many prefer to err on the side of safety and retest annually.

It is indeed fortunate that heartworm is relatively easy to prevent, because treatments can be as life-threatening as the disease itself. Treatment requires a two-step process that kills the adult heartworms first and then the microfilariae. Prevention is obviously preferable; this involves a once-monthly oral or topical treatment. The most common oral preventives include ivermectin (not suitable for some breeds), moxidectin and milbe-mycin oxime; the once-a-month topical drug selamectin provides heartworm protection in addition to flea, some types of tick and other parasite controls.

THE **ABC**S OF

Emergency Care

Abrasions

Clean wound with running water or 3% hydrogen peroxide. Pat dry with gauze and spray with antibiotic. Do not cover.

Animal Bites

Clean area with soap and saline solution or water. Apply pressure to any bleeding area. Apply antibiotic ointment. Identify biting animal and contact the vet.

Antifreeze Poisoning

Induce vomiting and take dog to the vet.

Bee Sting

Remove stinger and apply soothing lotion or cold compress; give antihistamine in proper dosage.

Bleeding

Apply pressure directly to wound with gauze or towel for five to ten minutes. If wound does not stop bleeding, wrap wound with gauze and adhesive tape.

Bloat/Gastric Torsion

Immediately take the dog to the vet or emergency clinic; phone from car. No time to waste.

Burns

Chemical: Bathe dog with water and pet shampoo. Rinse in saline solution. Apply antibiotic ointment.

Acid: Rinse with water. Apply one part baking soda, two parts water to affected area.

Alkali: Rinse with water. Apply one part vinegar, four parts water to affected area.

Electrical: Apply antibiotic ointment. Seek veterinary assistance immediately.

Choking

If the dog is on the verge of collapsing, wedge a solid object, such as the handle of a screwdriver, between molars on one side of mouth to keep mouth open. Pull tongue out. Use long-nosed pliers or fingers to remove foreign object. Do not push the object down the dog's throat. For small or medium dogs, hold dog upside down by hind legs and shake firmly to dislodge foreign object.

Chlorine Ingestion

With clean water, rinse the mouth and eyes. Give dog water to drink; contact the vet.

Constipation

Feed dog 2 tablespoons bran flakes with each meal. Encourage drinking water. Mix 1/4-teaspoon mineral oil in dog's food. Contact vet if persists longer than 24 hours.

Diarrhea

Withhold food for 12 to 24 hours. Feed dog anti-diarrheal with eyedropper. When feeding resumes, feed one part boiled hamburger, one part plain cooked rice, 1/4- to 3/4-cup four times daily. Contact vet if persists longer than 24 hours.

Dog Bite

Snip away hair around puncture wound; clean with 3% hydrogen peroxide; apply tincture of iodine. Identify biting dog and call the vet. If wound appears deep, take the dog to the vet.

Frostbite

Wrap the dog in a heavy blanket. Warm affected area with a warm bath for ten minutes. Red color to skin will return with circulation; if tissues are pale after 20 minutes, contact the vet.

Use a portable, durable container large enough to contain all items.

DOG OWNER'S FIRST-AID KIT

❏ **Gauze bandages/swabs**
❏ **Adhesive and non-adhesive bandages**
❏ **Antibiotic powder**
❏ **Antiseptic wash**
❏ **Hydrogen peroxide 3%**
❏ **Antibiotic ointment**
❏ **Lubricating jelly**
❏ **Rectal thermometer**
❏ **Nylon muzzle**
❏ **Scissors and forceps**
❏ **Eyedropper**
❏ **Syringe**
❏ **Anti-bacterial/fungal solution**
❏ **Saline solution**
❏ **Antihistamine**
❏ **Cotton balls**
❏ **Nail clippers**
❏ **Screwdriver/pen knife**
❏ **Flashlight**
❏ **Emergency phone numbers**

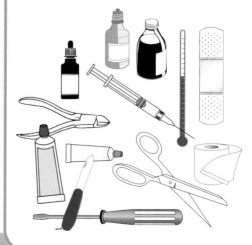

Heat Stroke
Submerge the dog (up to his muzzle) in cold water; if no response within ten minutes, contact the vet.

Hot Spots
Mix 2 packets Domeboro® with 2 cups water. Saturate cloth with mixture and apply to hot spots for 15–30 minutes. Apply antibiotic ointment. Repeat every six to eight hours.

Poisonous Plants
Wash affected area with soap and water. Cleanse with alcohol. For foxtail/grass, apply antibiotic ointment. Contact vet if plant was ingested.

Rat Poison Ingestion
Induce vomiting. Keep dog calm, maintain dog's normal body temperature (use blanket or heating pad). Get to the vet for antidote.

Shock
Keep the dog calm and warm; call for veterinary assistance.

Snake Bite
If possible, bandage the area and apply pressure. If the area is not conducive to bandaging, use ice to control bleeding. Get immediate help from the vet.

Tick Removal
Apply flea and tick spray directly on tick. Wait one minute. Using tweezers or wearing plastic gloves, grasp the tick's body firmly and pull out. Apply antibiotic ointment.

Vomiting
Restrict water intake; offer a few ice cubes. Withhold food for next meal. Contact vet if vomiting persists longer than 24 hours.

Curly-Coats are robust dogs, often remaining quite active in their senior years.

CURLY-COATED RETRIEVER

When we bring home a puppy, full of the energy and exuberance that accompanies youth, we hope for a long, happy and fulfilling relationship with the new family member. Even when we adopt an older dog, we look forward to the years of companionship ahead with a new canine friend. However, aging is inevitable for all creatures, and there will come a time when your Curly-Coated Retriever reaches his senior years and will need special considerations and attention to his care.

In general, pure-bred dogs are considered to have achieved senior status when they reach 75% of their breed's average lifespan, with lifespan being based generally on breed size along with factors unique to each breed. Your Curly-Coated Retriever has an average lifespan of 10–12 and thus is a senior citizen at around 7 or 8.

Obviously, the old "seven dog years to one human year" theory is not exact. In puppyhood, a dog's year is actually comparable to more than seven human years, considering the puppy's rapid growth during his first year. Then, in adulthood, the ratio decreases. Further, the Curly's curve of

comparison is unique in that he is not considered physically mature until three to four years old. Regardless, the more viable rule of thumb is that the larger the dog, the shorter his expected lifespan. Of course, this can vary among individual dogs, with many living longer than expected, which we hope is the case and which is certainly possible with healthy, well-cared-for dogs.

By the time your dog has reached his senior years, you will know him very well, so the physical and behavioral changes that accompany aging should be noticeable to you. Humans and dogs share the most obvious physical sign of aging: gray hair! Graying often occurs first on the

Dogs and people share one of the most visible signs of aging—gray hair. Graying on the muzzle is the classic sign of the dog's "golden years."

muzzle and face, around the eyes. Another telltale sign is the dog's overall decrease in activity. Your older dog might be more content to nap and rest, and he may not show the same old enthusiasm when it's time to play in the yard or go for a walk. Other physical signs include significant weight loss or gain; more labored movement; skin and coat problems, possibly hair loss; sight and/or hearing problems; changes in toileting habits, perhaps seeming "unhousebroken" at times; tooth decay, bad breath or other mouth problems.

There are behavioral changes that go along with aging, too. There are numerous causes for behavioral changes. Sometimes a dog's apparent confusion results from a physical change like diminished sight or hearing. If his confusion causes him to be afraid, he may act aggressively or defensively. He may sleep more frequently because his daily walks, though shorter now, tire him out. He may begin to experience separation anxiety or, conversely, become less interested in petting and attention.

There also are clinical conditions that cause behavioral changes in older dogs. One such condition is known as canine cognitive dysfunction (familiarly known as "old-dog" syndrome). It can be frustrating for an owner whose dog is affected with cogni-

tive dysfunction, as it can result in behavioral changes of all types, most seemingly unexplainable. Common changes include the dog's forgetting aspects of the daily routine, such as times to eat, go out for walks, relieve himself and the like. Along the same lines, you may take your dog out at the regular time for a potty trip and he may have no idea why he is there. Sometimes a placid dog will begin to show aggressive or possessive tendencies or, conversely, a hyperactive dog will start to "mellow out."

Disease also can be the cause of behavioral changes in senior dogs. Hormonal problems (Cushing's disease is common in older dogs), diabetes and thyroid disease can cause increased appetite, which can lead to aggression related to food guarding. It's better to be proactive with your senior dog, making more frequent trips to the vet if necessary and having bloodwork done to test for the diseases that can commonly befall older dogs.

This is not to say that, as dogs age, they all fall apart physically and become nasty in personality. The aforementioned changes are discussed to alert owners to the things that may happen as their dogs get older. Many hardy dogs remain active and alert well into old age. However, it can be frustrating and heartbreaking for owners to see their beloved dogs

Number-One Killer Disease in Dogs: CANCER

In every age, there is a word associated with a disease or plague that causes humans to shudder. In the 21st century, that word is "cancer." Just as cancer is the leading cause of death in humans, it claims nearly half the lives of dogs that die from a natural disease as well as half the dogs that die over the age of ten years.

Described as a genetic disease, cancer becomes a greater risk as the dog ages. Vets and dog owners have become increasingly aware of the threat of cancer to dogs. Statistics reveal that one dog in every five will develop cancer, the most common of which is skin cancer. Many cancers, including prostate, ovarian and breast cancer, can be avoided by spaying and neutering our dogs by the age of six months.

Early detection of cancer can save or extend a dog's life, so it is absolutely vital for owners to have their dogs examined by a qualified vet or oncologist immediately upon detection of any abnormality. Certain dietary guidelines have also proven to reduce the onset and spread of cancer. Foods based on fish rather than beef, due to the presence of Omega-3 fatty acids, are recommended. Other amino acids such as glutamine have significant benefits for canines, particularly those breeds that show a greater susceptibility to cancer.

Cancer management and treatments promise hope for future generations of canines. Since the disease is genetic, breeders should never breed a dog whose parents, grandparents and any related siblings have developed cancer. It is difficult to know whether to exclude an otherwise healthy dog from a breeding program, as the disease does not manifest itself until the dog's senior years.

RECOGNIZE CANCER WARNING SIGNS

Since early detection can possibly rescue your dog from becoming a cancer statistic, it is essential for owners to recognize the possible signs and seek the assistance of a qualified professional.

- Abnormal bumps or lumps that continue to grow
- Bleeding or discharge from any body cavity
- Persistent stiffness or lameness
- Recurrent sores or sores that do not heal
- Inappetence
- Breathing difficulties
- Weight loss
- Bad breath or odors
- General malaise and fatigue
- Eating and swallowing problems
- Difficulty urinating and defecating

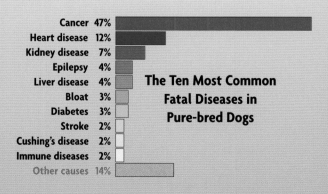

Disease	%
Cancer	47%
Heart disease	12%
Kidney disease	7%
Epilepsy	4%
Liver disease	4%
Bloat	3%
Diabetes	3%
Stroke	2%
Cushing's disease	2%
Immune diseases	2%
Other causes	14%

The Ten Most Common Fatal Diseases in Pure-bred Dogs

A hardy and active dog, the Curly-Coated Retriever is the choice of discriminating dog folk seeking a highly trainable, responsive companion. This 11-year-old senior is still working.

change physically and temperamentally. Just know that it's the same Curly-Coated Retriever under there, and that he still loves you and appreciates your care, which he needs now more than ever.

Again, every dog is an individual in terms of aging. Your dog might reach the estimated "senior" age for his breed and show no signs of slowing down. However, even if he shows no outward signs of aging, he should begin a senior-care program. He may not show it, but he's not a pup anymore! By providing him with extra attention to his veterinary care at this age, you will be practicing good preventive medicine, ensuring that the rest of your dog's life will be as long, active, happy and healthy as possible. If you do notice indications of aging, such as graying and/or changes in sleeping, eating or toileting habits, this is a sign to

set up a senior-care visit with your vet right away to make sure that these changes are not related to any health problems.

To start, senior dogs should visit the vet twice yearly for exams, routine tests and overall evaluations. Many veterinarians have special screening programs especially for senior dogs that can include a thorough physical exam; blood test to determine complete blood count; serum biochemistry test, which screens for liver, kidney and blood problems as well as cancer; urinalysis; and dental exams. With these tests, it can be determined whether your dog has any health problems; the results also establish a baseline for your pet against which future test results can be compared.

In addition to these tests, your vet may suggest additional testing, including an EKG, tests for glaucoma and other problems of the eye, chest x-rays, screening for tumors, blood pressure test, test for thyroid function and screening for parasites and reassessment of his preventive program. Your vet also will ask you questions about your dog's diet and activity level, what you feed and the amounts that you feed. This information, along with his evaluation of the dog's overall condition, will enable him to suggest proper dietary changes, if needed.

This may seem like quite a work-up for your pet, but veterinarians advise that older dogs need more frequent attention so that any health problems can be detected as early as possible. Serious conditions like kidney disease, heart disease and cancer may not present outward symptoms, or the problem may go undetected if the symptoms are mistaken by owners as just part of the aging process.

There are some conditions more common in elderly dogs that are difficult to ignore. Cognitive dysfunction shares much in common with senility and Alzheimer's disease, and dogs are not immune. Dogs can become confused and/or disoriented, lose their house-training, have abnormal sleep-wake cycles and interact differently with their owners. Be heartened by the fact that, in some ways, there are more treatment options for dogs with cognitive dysfunction than for people with similar conditions. There is good evidence that continued stimulation in the form of games, play, training and exercise can help to maintain cognitive function. There are also medications (such as seligiline) and antioxidant-fortified senior diets that have been shown to be beneficial.

Cancer is also a condition more common in the elderly. While lung cancer, which is a major killer in humans, is relatively rare in dogs, almost all of the cancers seen in people are also seen in pets. If pets are getting

regular physical examinations, cancers are often detected early. There are a variety of cancer therapies available today, and many pets continue to live happy lives with appropriate treatment.

Degenerative joint disease, often referred to as arthritis, is another malady common to both elderly dogs and humans. A lifetime of wear and tear on joints and running around at play eventually takes its toll and results in stiffness and difficulty in getting around. As dogs live longer and healthier lives, it is natural that they should eventually feel some

SYMPTOMS OF SENILITY

Senility, cognitive dysfunction, mental deterioration, whatever you call it, many dogs experience it as they age. Be aware of changes in your dog, including confusion, in which your dog may fail to recognize you or other family members and/or wander aimlessly around the house; changes in barking patterns or barking for no apparent reason; changes in sleeping habits, such as sleeping during the day and being awake overnight; having toilet accidents in the house or not knowing what to do when you take him out for potty breaks; changes in his temperament and the like. Your vet may prescribe medications or suggest changes you can make around the home and in your routine to make your dog more comfortable.

of the effects of aging. Once again, if regular veterinary care has been available, your pet should not have been carrying extra pounds all those years and wearing those joints out before their time. If your pet was unfortunate enough to inherit hip dysplasia, osteochondritis dissecans or any of the other developmental orthopedic diseases, battling the onset of degenerative joint disease was probably a longstanding goal. In any case, there are now many

effective remedies for managing degenerative joint disease and a number of remarkable surgeries as well. If your dog is arthritic, gently massaging him each day can help decrease his joint pain with the added benefit of helping you detect any lumps, bumps or other abnormalities.

Aside from the extra veterinary care, there is much you can do at home to keep your older dog in good condition. The dog's diet is an important factor. If your dog's appetite decreases, he will not be getting the nutrients he needs. He also will lose weight, which is unhealthy for a dog at a proper weight. Conversely, an older dog's metabolism is slower and he usually exercises less, but he should not be allowed to become obese. Obesity in an older dog is especially risky, because extra pounds mean extra stress on the body, increasing his vulnerability to heart disease. Additionally, the extra pounds make it harder for the dog to move about.

You should discuss age-related feeding changes with your vet. For a dog who has lost interest in food, it may be suggested to try some different types of food until you find something new that he likes. For an obese dog, a "light"-formula dog food or reducing food portions may be advised, along with exercise appropriate to his physical condition and energy level.

COPING WITH A BLIND DOG

Blindness is one of the unfortunate realities of growing old, for both dogs and humans. Owners of blind dogs should not give up hope, as most dogs adapt to their compromised state with grace and patience. A sudden loss of sight poses more stress on the dog than a gradual loss, such as that through cataracts. Some dogs may need your assistance to help them get around; others will move around seemingly uninhibited. Owners may need to retrain the dog to handle some basic tasks. Teaching commands like "Wait," "Stop" and "Slow" are handy as you help the dog learn to maneuver around his world. You are now more than the team captain, you're the coach and cheerleader! If your blind dog is showing signs of depression, it is your job to encourage him and give him moral support, just as you might for a member of your family or a good friend.

As for exercise, the senior dog should not be allowed to become a "couch potato" despite his old age. He may not be able to handle the morning run, long walks and vigorous games of fetch, but he still needs to get up and get moving. Keep up with your daily walks, but keep the distances shorter and let your dog set the pace. If he gets to the point where he's not up for walks around the neighborhood, stroll around the yard with him. On the other hand, many dogs remain active in their senior years, so base changes to the exercise program on your own individual dog and what he's capable of. Don't worry, your Curly-Coated Retriever will let you know when it's time to rest.

Keep up with your grooming routine as you always have. Be extra-diligent about checking the skin and coat for problems. Older dogs can experience thinning coats as a normal aging process, but they can also lose hair as a result of medical problems. Some thinning is normal, but patches of baldness or the loss of significant amounts of hair is not.

Hopefully, you've been regular with brushing your dog's teeth throughout his life. Healthy teeth directly affect overall good health. We already know that bacteria from gum infections can enter the dog's body through the damaged gums and travel to the organs. At a stage in life when his organs

> **ACCIDENT ALERT!**
> Just as we puppy-proof our homes for the new member of the family, we must accident-proof our homes for the older dog. You want to create a safe environment in which the senior dog can get around easily and comfortably, with no dangers. A dog that slips and falls in old age is much more prone to injury than an adult, making accident prevention even more important. Likewise, dogs are more prone to falls in old age, as they do not have the same balance and coordination that they once had. Throw rugs on hardwood floors are slippery and pose a risk; even a throw rug on a carpeted surface can be an obstacle for the senior dog. Consider putting down non-slip surfaces or confining your dog to carpeted rooms.

don't function as well as they used to, you don't want anything to put additional strain on them. Clean teeth also contribute to a healthy immune system. Offering the dental-type chews in addition to toothbrushing can help, as they remove plaque and tartar as the dog chews.

Along with the same good care you've given him all of his life, pay a little extra attention to your dog in his senior years and keep up with at least twice-yearly trips to the vet. The sooner a problem is uncovered, the greater the chances of a full recovery.

CURLY-COATED RETRIEVER

Is dog showing in your blood? Are you excited by the idea of gaiting your handsome Curly-Coated Retriever around the ring to the thunderous applause of an enthusiastic audience? Are you certain that your beloved Curly-Coated Retriever is flawless? You are not alone! Every loving owner thinks that his dog has no faults, or too few to mention. No matter how many times an owner reads the breed standard, he cannot find any faults in his aristocratic companion dog. If this sounds like you, and if you are considering entering your Curly-Coated Retriever in a dog show, here are some basic questions to ask yourself:

• Did you purchase a "show-quality" puppy from the breeder?
• Is your puppy at least six months of age?
• Does the puppy exhibit correct show type for his breed?
• Does your puppy have any disqualifying faults?
• Is your Curly-Coated Retriever registered with the American Kennel Club?
• How much time do you have to devote to training, grooming, conditioning and exhibiting your dog?

• Do you understand the rules and regulations of a dog show?
• Do you have time to learn how to show your dog properly?
• Do you have the financial resources to invest in showing your dog?
• Will you show the dog yourself or hire a professional handler?
• Do you have a vehicle that can accommodate your weekend trips to the dog shows?

Success in the show ring requires more than a pretty face, a waggy tail and a pocketful of liver. Even though dog shows can be exciting and enjoyable, the sport of conformation makes great demands on the exhibitors and the dogs. Winning exhibitors live for their dogs, devoting time and money to their dogs' presentation, conditioning and training. Very few novices, even those with good dogs, will find themselves in the

AKC GROUPS
For showing purposes, the American Kennel Club divides its recognized breeds into seven groups: Sporting Dogs, Hounds, Working Dogs, Terriers, Toys, Non-Sporting Dogs and Herding Dogs.

winners' circle, though it does happen. Don't be disheartened, though. Every exhibitor began as a novice and worked his way up to the Group ring. It's the "working your way up" part that you must keep in mind.

Assuming that you have purchased a puppy of the correct type and quality for showing, let's begin to examine the world of showing and what's required to get started. Although the entry fee into a dog show is nominal, there are lots of other hidden costs involved with "finishing" your Curly-Coated Retriever, that is, making him a champion. Things like equipment, travel, training and conditioning all cost money. A more serious campaign will include fees for a professional handler, boarding, cross-country travel and advertising. Top-winning show dogs can represent a very considerable investment— over $100,000 has been spent in campaigning some dogs. (The investment can be less, of course, for owners who don't use professional handlers.)

Many owners, on the other hand, enter their "average" Curly-Coated Retrievers in dog shows for the fun and enjoyment of it. Dog showing makes an absorbing hobby, with many rewards for dogs and owners alike. If you're having fun, meeting other people who share your interests and enjoying the overall experience,

you likely will catch the "bug." Once the dog-show bug bites, its effects can last a lifetime; it's certainly much better than a deer tick! Soon you will be envisioning yourself in the center ring at the Westminster Kennel Club Dog Show in New York City, competing for the prestigious Best in Show cup. This magical dog show is televised annually from Madison Square Garden, and the victorious dog becomes a celebrity overnight.

AKC CONFORMATION BASICS
Visiting a dog show as a spectator is a great place to start. Pick up

Now retired from the show ring but still competing in field trials, Ch. Fairway It's My Party is a record-breaker and a top-winning Curly in the US.

to head in the ring for the Best in Show award.

What most spectators don't understand is the basic idea of conformation. A dog show is often referred as a "conformation" show. This means that the judge should decide how each dog stacks up (conforms) to the breed standard for his given breed: how well does this Curly-Coated Retriever conform to the ideal representative detailed in the standard? Ideally, this is what happens. In reality, however, this ideal often gets slighted as the judge compares Curly-Coated

A dog's gait is evaluated in the show ring, as a dog cannot move properly without proper body construction.

the show catalog to find out what time your breed is being shown, who is judging the breed and in which ring the classes will be held. To start, Curly-Coated Retrievers compete against other Curly-Coated Retrievers, and the winner is selected as Best of Breed by the judge. This is the procedure for each breed. At a group show, all of the Best of Breed winners go on to compete for Group One in their respective groups. For example, all Best of Breed winners in a given group compete against each other; this is done for all seven groups. Finally, all seven group winners go head

FIVE CLASSES AT SHOWS

At most AKC all-breed shows, there are five regular classes offered: Puppy, Novice, Bred-by-Exhibitor, American-bred and Open. The Puppy Class is usually divided as 6 to 9 months of age and 9 to 12 months of age. When deciding in which class to enter your dog, whether male or female, you must carefully check the show schedule to make sure that you have selected the right class. Depending on the age of the dog, previous first-place wins and the sex of the dog, you must make the best choice. It is possible to enter a one-year-old dog who has not won sufficient first places in any of the non-Puppy Classes, though the competition is more intense the further you progress from the Puppy Class.

Retriever #1 to Curly-Coated Retriever #2. Again, the ideal is that each dog is judged based on his merits in comparison to his breed standard, not in comparison to the other dogs in the ring. It is easier for judges to compare dogs of the same breed to decide which they think is the better specimen; in the Group and Best in Show ring, however, it is very difficult to compare one breed to another, like apples to oranges. Thus the dog's conformation to the breed standard—not to mention advertising dollars and good handling—is essential to success in conformation shows. The dog described in the standard (the standard for each AKC breed is written and approved by the breed's national parent club and then submitted to the AKC for approval) is the

The judge reviews the line-up of dogs to compare each to the breed standard, not to each other.

perfect dog of that breed, and breeders keep their eye on the standard when they choose which dogs to breed, hoping to get closer and closer to the ideal with each litter.

Another good first step for the novice is to join a dog club. You will be astonished by the many and different kinds of dog clubs in the country, with about 5,000 clubs holding events every year. Most clubs require that prospective new members present two letters of recommendation from existing members. Perhaps you've made some friends visiting a show held by a particular club and you would like to join that club. Dog clubs may specialize in a single breed, like a local or regional Curly-Coated Retriever club, or in a specific pursuit, such as obedience, tracking or hunting tests. There are all-breed clubs for all dog enthusiasts; they sponsor

BECOMING A CHAMPION

An official AKC championship of record requires that a dog accumulate 15 points under three different judges, including two "majors" under different judges. Points are awarded based on the number of dogs entered into competition, varying from breed to breed and place to place. A win of three, four or five points is considered a "major." The AKC annually assigns a schedule of points to adjust to the variations that accompany a breed's popularity and the population of a given area.

special training days, seminars on topics like grooming or handling or lectures on breeding or genetics. There are also clubs that specialize in certain types of dogs, like herding dogs, hunting dogs, companion dogs, etc.

A parent club is the national organization, sanctioned by the AKC, which promotes and safeguards its breed in the country. The Curly-Coated Retriever Club of America was formed in 1979 and can be contacted on the Internet at www.ccrca.org. The parent club holds an annual national specialty show, usually in a different city each year, in which many of the country's top dogs, handlers and breeders gather to compete. At a specialty show, only members of a single breed are invited to participate. There are also group specialties, in which all members of a group are invited (the Curly is a member of the Sporting Group). For more information about dog clubs in your area, contact the AKC at www.akc.org on the Internet or write them at their Raleigh, NC address.

MEET THE AKC

The American Kennel Club is the main governing body of the dog sport in the United States. Founded in 1884, the AKC consists of 500 or more independent dog clubs plus 4,500 affiliated clubs, all of which follow the AKC rules and regulations. Additionally, the AKC maintains a registry for pure-bred dogs in the US and works to preserve the integrity of the sport and its continuation in the country. Over 1,000,000 dogs are registered each year, representing about 150 recognized breeds. There are over 15,000 competitive events held annually for which over 2,000,000 dogs enter to participate. Dogs compete to earn over 40 different titles, from Champion to Companion Dog to Master Agility Champion.

OTHER TYPES OF COMPETITION

In addition to conformation shows, the AKC holds a variety of other competitive events. Obedience trials, agility trials and tracking trials are open to all breeds, while hunting tests, field trials, lure coursing, herding tests and trials, earthdog tests and coonhound events are limited to specific breeds or groups of breeds. The Junior Showmanship Program is offered to aspiring young handlers and their dogs, and the Canine Good Citizen® Program is an all-around good-behavior test open to all dogs, pure-bred and mixed.

OBEDIENCE TRIALS

Mrs. Helen Whitehouse Walker, a Standard Poodle fancier, can be credited with introducing obedience trials to the United

States. In the 1930s she designed a series of exercises based on those of the Associated Sheep, Police, Army Dog Society of Great Britain. These exercises were intended to evaluate the working relationship between dog and owner. Since those early days of the sport in the US, obedience trials have grown more and more popular, and now more than 2,000 trials each year attract over 100,000 dogs and their owners. Any dog registered with the AKC, regardless of neutering or other disqualifications that would preclude entry in conformation competition, can participate in obedience trials.

There are three levels of difficulty in obedience competition. The first (and easiest) level is the Novice, in which dogs can earn the Companion Dog (CD) title. The intermediate level is the Open level, in which the Companion Dog Excellent (CDX) title is awarded. The advanced level is the Utility level, in which dogs compete for the Utility Dog (UD) title. Classes at each level are further divided into "A" and "B," with "A" for beginners and "B" for those with more experience.

In order to win a title at a given level, a dog must earn three "legs." A "leg" is accomplished when a dog scores 170 or higher (200 is a perfect score). The scoring system gets a little trickier

when you understand that a dog must score more than 50% of the points available for each exercise in order to actually earn the points. Available points for each exercise range between 20 and 40.

Once he's earned the UD title, a dog can go on to win the prestigious title of Utility Dog Excellent (UDX) by winning "legs" in ten shows. Additionally, Utility Dogs who win "legs" in Open B and Utility B earn points toward the lofty title of Obedience Trial Champion (OTCh.). Established in 1977 by the AKC, this title requires a dog to earn 100 points as well as three first places in a

The judge goes over each dog with hands-on evaluation to feel for, not just look for, correct body structure.

The weave poles in an agility trial require speed, coordination and accuracy.

Agility trials became sanctioned by the AKC in August 1994, when the first licensed agility trials were held. Since that time, agility certainly has grown in popularity by leaps and bounds, literally! The AKC allows all registered breeds (including Miscellaneous Class breeds) to participate, providing the dog is 12 months of age or older. Agility is designed so that the handler demonstrates how well the dog can work at his side. The handler directs his dog through, over, under and around an obstacle course that includes jumps, tires, the dog walk, weave poles, pipe tunnels, collapsed tunnels and more. While working his way through the course, the dog must keep one eye and ear on the handler and the rest of his body on the course. The handler runs along with the dog, giving verbal and hand signals to guide the dog through the course.

The first organization to promote agility trials in the US was the United States Dog Agility Association, Inc. (USDAA). Established in 1986, the USDAA sparked the formation of many member clubs around the country. To participate in USDAA trials, dogs must be at least 18 months of age. The USDAA and AKC both offer titles to winning dogs, although the exercises and requirements of the two organizations differ.

combination of Open B and Utility B classes under three different judges. The "brass ring" of obedience competition is the AKC's National Obedience Invitational. This is an exclusive competition for only the cream of the obedience crop. In order to qualify for the invitational, a dog must be ranked in either the top 25 all-breeds in obedience or in the top 3 for his breed in obedience. The title at stake here is that of National Obedience Champion (NOC).

Agility trials are a great way to keep your dog active, and they will keep you running, too! You should join a local agility club to learn more about the sport. These clubs offer sessions in which you can introduce your dog to the various obstacles as well as training classes to prepare him for competition. In no time, your dog will be climbing A-frames, crossing the dog walk and flying over hurdles, all with you right beside him. Your heart will leap every time your dog jumps through the hoop—and you'll be having just as much (if not more) fun!

TRACKING

Tracking tests are exciting ways to test your Curly-Coated Retriever's instinctive scenting ability on a competitive level. All dogs have a nose, and all breeds are welcome in tracking tests. The first AKC-licensed tracking test took place in 1937 as part of the Utility level at an obedience trial, and thus competitive tracking was officially begun. The first title, Tracking Dog (TD), was offered in 1947, ten years after the first official tracking test. It was not until 1980 that the AKC added the title Tracking Dog Excellent (TDX), which was followed by the title Versatile Surface Tracking (VST) in 1995. Champion Tracker (CT) is awarded to a dog who has earned all three of those titles.

The TD level is the first and most basic level in tracking, progressing in difficulty to the TDX and then the VST. A dog must follow a track laid by a human 30 to 120 minutes prior in order to earn the TD title. The track is about 500 yards long and contains up to 5 directional changes. At the next level, the TDX, the dog must follow a 3- to 5-hour-old track over a course that is up to 1,000 yards long and has

Flying high over a bar jump on an agility trial! It's easy to see why agility is so much fun for dogs and their handlers.

up to 7 directional changes. In the most difficult level, the VST, the track is up to five hours old and located in an urban setting.

FIELD TRIALS

Field trials are offered to the retrievers, pointers and spaniel breeds of the Sporting Group as well as to the Beagles, Dachshunds and Bassets of the Hound Group. The purpose of field trials is to demonstrate a dog's ability to perform his breed's original purpose in the field. The events vary depending on the type of dog, but in all trials dogs compete against one another for placement and for points toward their Field Champion (FC) titles. Dogs that earn their FC titles plus their championship in the conformation ring are known as Dual Champions; this is extremely prestigious, as it shows that the dog is the ideal blend of form and function, excelling in both areas.

Retriever field trials, designed to simulate "an ordinary day's shoot," are popular and likely the most demanding of these trials. Dogs must "mark" the location of downed feathered game and then return the birds to the shooter. Successful dogs are able to "mark" the downed game by remembering where the bird fell as well as correct use of the wind and terrain. Dogs are tested both on land and in water.

Difficulty levels are based on the number of birds downed as well as the number of "blind retrieves" (where a bird is placed away from the view of the dog and the handler directs the dog by the use of hand signals and verbal commands). The term "Non-Slip" retriever, often applied to these trials, refers to a

CANINE GOOD CITIZEN® PROGRAM

Have you ever considered getting your dog "certified"? The AKC's Canine Good Citizen® Program affords your dog just that opportunity. Your dog shows that he is a well-behaved canine citizen, using the basic training and good manners you have taught him, by taking a series of ten tests that illustrate that he can behave properly at home, in a public place and around other dogs. The tests are administered by participating dog clubs, colleges, 4-H clubs, Scouts and other community groups and are open to all pure-bred and mixed-breed dogs. Upon passing the ten tests, the suffix CGC is then applied to your dog's name.

The ten tests are: 1. Accepting a friendly stranger; 2. Sitting politely for petting; 3. Appearance and grooming; 4. Walking on a lead; 5. Walking through a group of people; 6. Sit, down and stay on command; 7. Coming when called; 8. Meeting another dog; 9. Calm reaction to distractions; 10. Separation from owner.

dog that is steady at the handler's side until commanded to go. Every field trial includes four stakes of increasing levels of difficulty. Each stake is judged by a team of two judges who look for many natural abilities, including steadiness, courage, style, control and training.

HUNTING TESTS

Hunting tests are not competitive like field trials, and participating dogs are judged against a standard, as in a conformation show. The first hunting tests were devised by the North American Hunting Retriever Association

In field trials dogs are tested on land and in water at various levels of difficulty. Here's Cleo returning with a downed duck.

(NAHRA) as an alternative to field trials for retriever owners to appreciate their dogs' natural innate ability in the field without the expense and pressure of a formal field trial. The intent of hunting tests is the same as that of field trials: to test the dog's ability in a simulated hunting scenario.

The AKC instituted its hunting tests in June 1985; since then, their popularity has grown tremendously. The AKC offers three titles at hunting tests, Junior Hunter (JH), Senior Hunter (SH) and Master Hunter (MH). Each title requires that the dog earn qualifying "legs" at the tests: the JH requiring four; the SH, five; and the MH, six. In addition to the AKC, the United Kennel Club also offers hunting tests through its affiliate club, the Hunting Retriever Club, Inc. (HRC), which began the tests in 1984.

FOR MORE INFORMATION...

For reliable up-to-date information about registration, dog shows and other canine competitions, contact one of the national registries by mail or via the Internet.

American Kennel Club
5580 Centerview Dr., Raleigh, NC 27606-3390
www.akc.org

United Kennel Club
100 E. Kilgore Road, Kalamazoo, MI 49002
www.ukcdogs.com

Canadian Kennel Club
89 Skyway Ave., Suite 100, Etobicoke, Ontario M9W 6R4, Canada
www.ckc.ca

The Kennel Club
1-5 Clarges St., Piccadilly, London W1Y 8AB, UK
www.the-kennel-club.org.uk

INDEX

Aarowag 16, 18
Ability 21, 23
Acetaminophen 59
Activities 24, 108
Activity level 21
—of senior dog 144
Addidas 17
Addidas Alpha Monopoly 18
Addidas Christmas Party 18
Addidas General Sherman 19
Adenovirus 120
Adult dog
—adoption of 86
—feeding 69
—health 111
—training 85-86
Aggression 21, 57, 65, 87, 102-103, 119
Agility 13, 19, 108
—trials 24, 150, 152
Aging 91, 113, 139
Akrow kennels 12
All-breed Best in Show 17
Aloofness 22
Alpha role 96
American Heartworm Society 135
American Kennel Club 16, 19, 146, 150, 155
—address 155
—Companion Animal Recovery 82
—competitive events 150
—conformation showing 147
—obedience competition 108
Ancylostoma caninum **131, 134**
Anderson, Jane 17
Anderson, Sheila 17
Anemia 72
Annual vet exams 113
Antifreeze 54, 115
Appetite loss 69, 115, 117
Arthritis 143
Ascarid **130**, 131
Ascaris lumbricoides **130**
Ashburton, Phillip 9
Attention 97-98, 104
Australia 9, 12-13, 14-15
Auto-immune deficiency 25
Avanti 17-18
Back Bay 16
Banworth 12
Banworth Athene 13
Banworth Ivurried 17
Banworth Simon 13
Barking 22
Bathing 23, 75, 77
Bedding 48, 56, 93
Behavior of senior dog 140
Bell, Thomas 11
Best in Show 17, 148-149
Best of Breed 148
Bielby, Walter 15
Bite 43
Biting 103
Blindness 144
Bloat 30, 71, 115
Body language 87, 94, 101
Body temperature 113
Bones 49, 70
Booster shots 54
Bordetella 120
Bordetella bronchiseptica 119
Boredom 21-22
Borrelia burgdorferi 120
Borreliosis 119
Bowls 46
Boyerie 17-18
Boyerie's Andouille O' Wits End 18
Bravery 13
Breed standard 43, 148

Breeder 26, 28, 43, 149
—early 10
—selection 39, 44, 110
—locating 39
British Quadrupeds 11
Brushing 75
Burtoncurl 12
Canadian Kennel Club 155
Cancer 119, 141, 143
Canine cough 120
Canine development schedule 91
Canine Eye Registration Foundation 30
Canine Good Citizen® Program 150, 154
Canis domesticus 10
Canis lupus 10
Car travel 83, 102
Carnsford Kyeema Patch 16
Champion Tracker 153
Charcol 12
Charwin 16-18
Charwin Scirocco 17
Chesapeake Bay Retriever 23
Chew toys 48, 50, 56, 61, 90, 93
Chewing 48, 56, 60, 102
Cheyletiella mite 127
Chicago 16
Chiggers 129
Children 21, 55, 57, 61, 63, 87, 102
Chow, Susan 18
Clippert, Conrad and Ann 19
Clubs 149
Coat 21, 23
—care 23, 75
—of senior dog 145
—insulation 23
Cognitive dysfunction 113, 143
Collar 51, 81, 97, 102
Color 23
Colostrum 12
Come 58, 102-104, 108
Commands 99-106
—potty 95
Commitment of ownership 40, 43, 45
Commoner's dog 13
Companion 21
Companion Dog 151
Companion Dog Excellent 151
Competitive events 150
Conference Table 16
Conformation shows 146-150
Consistency 51, 58, 61-62, 87-88
Coombehurst 12
Cooper, Yvonne 18
Core vaccines 119
Coronavirus 119-120
Corrections 97
Counter surfing 64
Courage 9, 13
Coventry 16
Crate 47, 49, 55-56, 64, 90, 92
—pads 48
—training 90-95
Crying 56, 63, 93
Ctenocephalides canis **122**
Curly-coated breeds 10
Curly-Coated Retriever Club of America 16, 39, 150
Cystitis 121
Dangers in the home 52, 54
Darelyn 12
Darelyn Aristocrat 12-13
Darelyn Rifleman 12
DEET 129
Degenerative joint disease 143
Delilah of Darelyn 12
Demodex mite 129
Demodicosis 128-129

Dental
—care of senior dog 145
—health 111, 113, 115, 117
—problems 69
Depression 144
Dese 18
Dese's Black As Coal 18
Dettweiler, Mr. Dale 15
Development of breed in England 10
Diet 70-71
—adult 69
—making changes 68
—puppy 67
—senior dog 72, 144
Digging 22, 64
Dilatation 71
Discipline 58-59, 95-96
Distemper 119-120
Distichiasis 28
Dipylidium caninum 132, **134**
Dirofilaria immitis 133, **134, 135**
Dog clubs 149
Dog flea 122
Dogfight 102
Dogs of Australia 15
Dominance 99, 107
Down 62, 94, 100-101
Down/stay 103
Drooling 25
Dru of Darelyn 12
Dry baths 77
Dual Champion 154
Dukes, Maryu 18
Ear
—cleaning 80
—mite infestation 80, 127-128
Echinococcus multilocularis 133
Eggs 70
El Mack 16
Elbow dysplasia 28
Emergency care 115
Endurance 24
Energy level 21, 23, 24
England 9-10, 12-13, 17
Entropion 28
Establishment of breed 9
Estrus 23, 119
Europe 13
Evans, Donald and Sonia 18
Excessive water intake 73, 121
Exercise 22, 24, 71, 73-74
—puppy 24
—senior dog 145
Exercise pen 90
Expenses of ownership 48
External parasites 122-129
Exuberance 21
Eye problems 28
Fairway 17-18
Fairway It's My Party **18, 147**
Fairway's Devilish Ace 19
Fairways Softmaple Finnheir 19
Family meeting the puppy 55
Fear 57
—aggression 103
—period 58
Feeding 65, 67-68, 70-71
—adult 69
—schedule 67
Fenced yard 22, 24, 54, 102
Field Champion 154
Field-trials 14, 19, 24, 109, 150, 154
First aid 115
First night in new home 56
Flat-Coated Retriever 11-12, 15
Fleas **122**, 123, **124**

Flyball 24, 109
Food 68, 70-71, 90
—bowls 46
—guarding 65
—loss of interest in 69, 115, 117
—poisonous to dogs 72
—raw 70
—rewards 85, 87, 89, 96, 106
Gastric torsion 30, 71, 115
Gastroplexy 71
Genetic testing 110
Gentleness 21
Giardia 120
Gladrags Jackaranda **13**
Gladrags Phorse Be With You 19
Gladrags USA 19
Golden Retriever 24
Gray wolf 10
Grinder for nails 78
Grinkle 12
Grooming 23, 77-78
Group competition 148-149
Gundog 9-10, 15, 21
—trials 109
Handler 146
Harkaway 12
Health 54
—adult 111
—benefits of dog ownership 27
—concerns 25
—journal 55
—puppy 41, 110
—senior dog 113, 142
Heart problems 30, 113
Heartworm 111, 133, **134, 135**
Heat cycle 23, 119
Heel 105-106
Hematuria 121
Hembrey, Mary Alice 17
Hepatitis 119-120
Herding events 150
Hereditary diseases 40
—of the eye 40
Heterodoxus spiniger 128
Hie-On Mack MacLaig **15**, 17
Hip dysplasia 26, 29, 144
Hodges, Doris 17
HomeAgain™ Companion Animal Retrieval System 82
Homemade toys 50
Hookworm **131, 134**
House-training 47, 61, 88-95
Hunting 24, 108
—dog 9-10, 13-14, 19
—Retriever Club 155
—tests 24, 150, 155
Identification 81
Independence 21
Infectious diseases 118
Insurance 44, 118
Intelligence 13-14, 21
Internal parasites 130-135
International Kennel Club 16
Irish Water Spaniel 9-10
Irishit Straight Line 12
Ixodes dammini **125-126**
Jangio's Lightning Bug 19
Jar-em 16
Jollybodies 16-17
Jumping up 62, 93
Junior Hunter 155
Junior Showmanship 150
Kangaroo 3
Karakul 16-17
Karakul Corona De Sombra 17
Karakul Titan **16**, 17-18
Karakul Trademark 18

Kennel Club, The
—address 155
—breed recognition 11
—classification of breed 11
—registrations 12
Kidney problems 113
Kiernan, Kim 18
Knysna 12
Kurly Kreek 17-18
Kurly Kreek Mae West 18
Kurly Kreek Marshall Dillon Boyerie 18, **19**
Kurly Kreek Stocking Stuffer 18
KyterCurl IDo What ILike 19
Labrador Retriever 11-12, 15, 23
Lakeview 16
Leash 51, 97
—pulling on 106
Leave it 102
Leptospirosis 119-120
Lifespan 113
Limey 15-17
Liver 70
Lizah Nero 16
Lost dog 81
Louse **128**
Loyalty 21-22
Lure coursing 150
Lyme disease 119
Mammary cancer 119
Marti, Janean 17-18
Martins Ravensdown Ben 15
Master Hunter 155
Mathel 16
Mathel Felicitation 18
Maturity rate 22, 28
Mayhem 16-17
Mayhem's Gentlemen's Agreement 17-18
Meat 70
Meat dog 11
Meek, Gary and Mary 17, 19
Mello, John 17
Memory 22
Methods of training 86
Microchip 82
Milk 70
Miscellaneous Class 152
Mites **127**, 128, **129**
Mounting 119
Mosquitoes 129, 133, 135
Multi-dog household 74
Murray River Curly 14
Nail clipping 77-78
Name 98, 104
National Obedience Champion 152
Nelson Prince 13
Nelson, Rita 19
Neutering 111, 119, 121
New Zealand 9, 12-14
Newfoundland 25
Nightflight 16
Nipping 60, 63
Non-core vaccines 119
North American Hunting Retriever Association 155
Notlaw 12
Obedience 25, 101
—classes 22, 97, 107
—Trial Champion 151
—trials 19, 24, 107, 150
Obesity 74, 144
Off 62, 65, 93
Okay 101, 106, 108
Old Water Dog 9
Onions 72
Origin 9
Orthopedic Foundation for Animals 27, 28
Orthopedic problems of senior dog 143
Osteochondritis dissecans 144
Other dogs 74, 119
Other pets 87
Otodectes cynotis 127
Outdoor safety 54
Ovariohysterectomy 121

Owner considerations 40
Ownership 40, 43, 45
—expenses of 48
—health benefits of 27
Pack animals 10, 58
Paper-training 88, 90, 94
Parainfluenza 119-120
Parasites 55
—control 111
—external 122-129
—internal 130-135
Parent club 150
Parvovirus 119-120
Patience 87
Patterned baldness 25
Pedigree 41, 43, 45
Pegasus 13
Penworthan 12
Perseverance 24
Personality 21
Physical characteristics 23
Pizzazz 17-18
Pizzazz Avanti Gonna Go Far 19
Plants 52, 115
Playtime 103
Poisons 52, 54, 59, 72, 115
Poodle 9-10
Popularity 11, 14, 19
Portuguese Water Dog **11**
Positive reinforcement 55, 88-89, 96, 99
Possessive behavior 65
Praise 85, 87, 89, 96, 107
Preston 12
Preventive care 110, 113, 115
Prince of Knocksginan 12
Professional help 103
Proglottid 133
Progressive retinal atrophy 30
Prostate problems 119
Ptarmigan 16-18
Ptarmigan Gale At Riverwatch **17**, 19
Ptarmigan Groovin 18
Pulling on leash 106
Punishment 64, 95-97
Puppy
—common problems 60
—diet 67
—establishing leadership 85
—exercise 24
—feeding 67
—first night in new home 56
—health 40, 41, 110
—kindergarten training class 98
—meeting the family 55
—needs 89
—parasites 55
—personality 45, 111
—proofing 52
—selection 39, 42, 44, 110
—show quality 43, 46, 146-147
—socialization 57
—supplies for 46
—teething 56, 61
—temperament 47
—training 57, 59, 85, 87
Pure-bred dogs 14
Rabies 119-120
Rally obedience 19
Ranah 16
Rawhide 49
Recognition of breed 11
Renniston 12
Retinal dysplasia 30
Retriever field trials 154
Retrievers 9, 11-12, 21, 23
—Curly-Coated 11
—Wavy Coated 11
Rewards 85, 87, 89, 95, 96, 106
Rhabditis **134**
Riverwatch 17-18
Riverwatch Desert Wind **20**
Riverwatch Quietly Makin Noiz 19
Riverwatch Southern Cross **19**, 33

Riverwatch Windwalker 19
Roaming 119
Rope toys 50
Roundworm 55, 130, 131, **134**
Routine 51, 61
Safety 47, 52, 59, 72, 83, 90, 93, 102-103
—commands 102
—for the older dog 145
—in the car 102
—outdoors 54
Sandbar 16-17
Sarcoptes scabiei **127**
Sarona Simon 13
Scabies 127
Scent attraction 94
Schedule 51, 61, 94
Scott, John 10
Senior dog 113
—behavioral changes 140
—dental care 145
—diet 72, 144
—exercise 145
—health 113
—safety 145
—signs of aging 139
—veterinary care 142
Senior Hunter 155
Sevenravens 16-17
Sevenravens Windbell 17
Sex differences 42
Shadowbrook 18
Shadowbrooks First PJ Party 19
Shedding 23, 75
Shifflet, Scott and Kathy 18
Shopping for puppy needs 46
Show-quality 43, 46, 146, 147
Shows
—conformation 146-150
—costs of 147
—first supported entry in US 16
—specialty 150
Siccawei 12
Siccawei Black Rod 15-16
Sit 99-100
Sit/stay 101
Size 21
Snaphill 12
Social tendencies 22
Socialization 22, 43, 57, 59, 65, 97-98, 111
Soft toys 49
Softmaple 17-18
Solimar 16
Sorona 12
Spaying 111, 119, 121
Specialty show 150
Sporting dogs 108
Sporting Group 17
Sportsman's Cabinet 9
Sportsman's Repository 10
Spot bath 77
St. John's Newfoundland 10
Standard 33, 43, 148
Stay 101, 106
Stomach stapling 71
Strangers 22
Stray dog 81
Strength 9
Stress 106
Summerwind 16, 18
Summerwind Echo's of Freedom 17
Summerwind's Charles Dickens **16**, 17
Sundevil Cerulean 19
Supervision 60-61, 93
Surgery 121
Swimming 23-24, 74-75
Table scraps 70
Taenia pisiformis 133
Tapeworm 132, **133**, **134**
Teeth 111, 115, 117
Teething 56, 61
Temperament 21, 47
—evaluation 111
Temperature, taking your dog's 113

Tenacity 9
Testicular cancer 119
Therapy dog 108
Thirst 73, 121
Tick-borne diseases 125
Ticks **125-126**
Timing 87, 89, 94, 103
Tokolics, Sue 17
Toxascaris leonine 130
Toxins 52, 54, 59, 70, 72, 115
Toxocara canis **130**
Toys 48, 50, 56, 61, 90, 93
Tracheobronchitis 120
Tracking 108, 150, 153
Tracking Dog 153
Tracking Dog Excellent 153
Training 21-22, 24, 61-63
—basic principles of 85, 87
—commands 99-106
—consistency in 58, 62, 88
—crate 90-95
—early 59
—importance of timing 94, 103
—methods 108
—practice 98
—proper attitude 96
—puppy 57, 87
—tips 60
Travel 47, 102
Treats 55, 69, 85, 87, 89, 96
—weaning off in training 106
Trichuris sp. **132**
Tricks 109
Trimming 76
Turkamann 12
Tweed Water Spaniel 10
Type 146-147
United Kennel Club 19, 155
—address 155
—obedience competition 108
United States 9, 12-14, 15
United States Dog Agility Association 152
Urinary tract problems 121
Urine marking 119
Utility Dog 151
Utility Dog Excellent 151
Vaccinations 54-55, 58, 111, 118, 119
Versatile Surface Tracking 153
Veterinarian 26, 39, 42, 49-50, 54, 102, 111, 113, 115
—care 25
—insurance 118
—specialties 117
Visiting the litter 44
Vitamin A toxicity 70
Voice 96
Volvulus 30, 71, 115
Vota, Delene and Henry 19
Wait 102
Waitoki Tamatakapua 13
Waitoki Tuhora 14
Walker, Mrs. Helen Whitehouse 150
Watchdog 22
Water 71-72, 90
—bowls 46
—increased intake 73, 121
Weight 23
West Nile virus 129
Westminster Kennel Club 17, 19, 147
Whining 56, 63, 93
Whipworm **132**
Windpatch 15
Windpatch Baron O'Goldendeed 16
Windpatch Demure Anne 17
Windpatch Devil O'Goldendeed 16
Windpatch Ebony Walkabout 16
Windpatch Nero's Lollipop 16
Windpatch Raven O'Goldendeed 16
Wit's End 16-17
Wolf 10
Working trials 109
World Wars 11, 12, 15
Worm control 55, 132
Yard 54

My Curly-Coated Retriever

PUT YOUR PUPPY'S FIRST PICTURE HERE

Dog's Name _____

Date _____ Photographer _____